SIMPLE STEPS
YOU CAN TAKE
TO SELL YOUR HOME
FASTER AND FOR MORE
MONEY IN ANY MARKET

SIMPLE STEPS YOU CAN TAKE TO SELL YOUR HOME FASTER AND FOR MORE MONEY IN ANY MARKET

Ilyce R. Glink

THREE RIVERS PRESS

NEW YORK

This book is intended as a general guide to the topics discussed and does not deliver accounting, personal finance, or legal advice. It is not intended, and should not be used, as a substitute for professional advice (legal or otherwise). You should consult a competent attorney and/or other professional with specific issues, problems, or questions you may have.

Company names, logos, and trademarks used in the book belong to the companies that own them. There is no attempt to appropriate these names, logos, and trademarks, and none should be construed. Also, there is no endorsement, implied or otherwise, of the companies listed in this book. They are used to illustrate the types of places, software, or information centers where readers can find more information. Finally, company names, phone numbers, addresses, and websites may have changed since the publication of this book.

For an up-to-date list of websites or to contact Ilyce Glink, please visit her website, www.thinkglink.com.

Published by Three Rivers Press, New York, New York.
Member of the Crown Publishing Group, a division of Random House, Inc.
www.randomhouse.com

THREE RIVERS PRESS and the Tugboat design are registered trademarks of Random House, Inc.

Printed in the United States of America

Library of Congress Cataloging-in-Publication Data

Glink, Ilyce R., 1964—
   50 simple steps you can take to sell your home faster and for more money in any market / Ilyce R. Glink.—1st ed.
Includes index.
   1. House selling.   I. Title: Fifty simple steps you can take to sell your home faster and for more money in any market.   II. Title.
   HD1379 .G578 2003
   333.33'83—dc21   2002151267

ISBN 0-609-80933-4

10 9 8 7 6 5 4 3 2 1

First Edition

For Sam, Alex, and Michael, who remind me every day
that the simple things in life are best

Contents

Preface

If buying a home seems scary, selling has the potential to really turn your world upside down. It's not just the physical work of packing up, keeping things clean, and making a fast getaway just before a prospective home buyer turns up. The emotional pain of separating from a place you've loved and where you've raised your family can be depressing, if not debilitating.

If you're going to sell, you'll have to separate from your home—and the sooner, the better. Until you do, you'll remain a homeowner rather than a home seller.

Of course, there's nothing wrong with being a homeowner. But it can get in the way of selling your home faster, and for more money. That's because as homeowners, we tend to overlook small things—like squeaky doors, rusty hinges, ripped window screens, and missing storm windows—that seem like a big deal to home buyers. They don't want to move into a home with peeling paint and bubbly wallpaper. They want to move into a home that's as close to being new as a fifteen-, twenty-, or forty-year-old home can be.

It's your job to give home buyers what they want, and to meet their (reasonable) expectations. If you do, you'll be amply rewarded: a faster sale, for more money—goals you can easily achieve in any market. *50 Simple Steps You Can Take to Sell Your Home Faster and for More Money in Any Market* is your guide to making the right moves when it comes to selling your home. For more detailed information on the home-selling process, including information on closing costs and fees and details about how the process of selling works, check out my other book for home sellers: *100 Questions Every Home Seller Should Ask*.

May you have wind in your sale.

Ilyce R. Glink
Summer 2002

P.S. If you'd like to ask a question, share a story, or are looking for more information, visit my Web site, www.thinkglink.com. I continually update the site with new information as it becomes available.

Introduction

After a while, your home becomes as comfortable and cozy as a blanket on a cool winter's night. You might do odd jobs here and there to keep things updated, or perhaps not. As the days and years pass, you might not notice that the paint has cracked and yellowed in the living room and that the bathroom wallpaper has begun to peel off in the corners. You'll hardly see the chip in the bathroom cabinet mirror, or the scraped-up oak floor in the dining room.

We learn to accept and eventually overlook most of the minor imperfections in our homes. Even the fixes of the most egregious imperfections get shunted aside by our hectic lives. If we didn't learn to live in our homes as they are, we'd go crazy trying to keep everything in perfect order. But just because we no longer see the imperfections doesn't mean they don't exist. They do, and they'll hurt you if you don't take care of them before you put your home on the market.

This book includes a series of simple steps designed to help you eliminate any potential problem a prospective buyer would encounter when considering whether your home is right for him or her. For example, many cash- and time-strapped home buyers don't allow ripped window screens to bother them. They see the rip, but fixing the problem isn't that simple. Like any job around the house, it could mean hours of time on the phone with the local home-improvement store, only to have to call the local storm window company, then to have to sit and figure out when the company can send out someone to retrieve the windows or install the new screens. And when it's all over, the time spent, not to mention the cost, of repairing a few window screens has left even the heartiest person drained. But left undone, it could become an obstacle to the swift sale of your home.

If buying a home is the single largest purchase you'll ever make, and if, over time, your home has appreciated in value and become your single biggest investment, when it comes time to sell, it makes sense to consider that you're unloading your single biggest asset. For most Americans, their home represents the largest portion of their net worth.

Maximizing your profit takes lots of planning and hard work. There aren't too many shortcuts—although I've included a few—in your quest to do it right. This book will help you get there.

Remember, your job as a seller is to meet the expectations that prospective buyers have about your property. If you want to max out your profit, you'll need to exceed their expectations, and you do that by presenting them with a home that's a showpiece.

Let's get going.

1

Five Rules Every Home Seller Should Live By

SIMPLE STEP

1

IF YOU KNOW SOMETHING'S BROKE, FIX IT!

Let's start out with a simple truth: Your home probably needs some, if not a lot of, work to prepare it for sale. This is true of any property, including mine. I have no plans to sell, but when I look around my own house, I can quickly spot at least a half-dozen items that would need fixing or finishing before I could sell, including installing the undercounter lights for the kitchen that we bought a year ago, painting a few pieces of trim that were somehow overlooked the last time the interior was painted, installing a screen on a window that's missing one, installing a path to our front door, and building a backyard patio (which, as we went to press, we decided to delay yet again because we still don't know what style and type of surface material we want to use).

Sometimes the loose ends are broken items that need repair. It irks home buyers to see something that's broken, like cracked tile or a wall clock that displays the wrong time because it needs a new set of batteries. Again, failing to fix broken items (especially those that can be easily repaired) sends a message to the buyer that you don't care enough to get these things done. Also, when the home inspector comes through (which he or she inevitably will do), you know these items will come up in the "need-to-do-before-I'll-close-on-your-house" list.

What should you fix? Anything that a prospective home buyer will think should be in working order on the day of sale, including:

- **All appliances.** They don't have to be new, but everything should work.

- **All faucets.** If it leaks or doesn't turn on correctly, repair or replace it.

- **All windows.** If any windowpanes are cracked, or don't open properly, fix or replace them. And make sure to repair all screen doors and windows.

- **All doors.** No creaking, no doors that open only partially, no cabinet doors that don't open at all.

- **Any exterior problems.** Replace missing roof shingles, repair your gutter if it has come apart, and regrade landscaping away from the house if you've been finding puddles or wet walls in your basement.

A GOOD START

Throughout this book, you'll need to keep paper and pencil handy to jot down different things. To make the job easier, purchase a small, inexpensive, spiral-bound notebook. This notebook, on which you'll spend less than a dollar, will become the nerve center of your home sale. You could keep a duplicate set of lists in your computer, but it's helpful to have something you can write on and work with while you're walking through the interior and around the exterior of your home.

Open up your notebook to the first page, and start touring your home. You'll want to walk all over the interior (including the basement, the garage, and the attic) and the exterior of your home, looking for anything that's broken. Pay special attention to the furnace (which, depending on its age, type, and condition, should be serviced once a year by a professional heating and air-conditioning expert—be sure it has been serviced within twelve months before you list your home), faucets and drains, and cracked tiles. Make a list of every single item that needs a repair, whether it's a small fix (adding oil to a squeaky door hinge) or peeling wallpaper in the guest bath.

Ideally, you should fix everything on this list before you sell. But just in case, be sure to prioritize the list so that you tackle the most important (i.e., *conspicuous*) problems first.

This list isn't for updating your home—although peeling wallpaper might count as decorating. Rather, you're specifically looking for items that are broken and need repair. The repairs stage is very different from what you'll do later, when you're decorating your home to show.

Once your list is assembled and prioritized, schedule the necessary repairs. You may need to call in a furnace cleaning and repair company. Or you may need an electrician or plumber. Get the best people you can afford so that the job is done right. And keep your receipts from all the tradespeople who helped you out.

Remember, your buyer isn't going to give you gold stars for the stuff that's supposed to be working in your home. But you certainly will get demerits for the stuff that doesn't.

Web Sites and Other Places to Find Help for Home Repairs

If you need to do work in your home before you sell, the best place to get a referral is to ask your parents, family members, or friends for a recommendation. (Be sure to ask if they liked the person who did the job, how much he or she charged, and if they'd have this individual do another job for them.) But if no one has any recommendations, you'll have to take it a Step further.

To get a referral for a home-related job, go online to Angieslist.com. You might also try AskTheBuilder.com, a site run by syndicated columnist and radio personality Tim Carter. There are other referral sites out there, but my readers have had luck with these two. Check my Web site, ThinkGlink.com, for updates to the referral Web sites list.

After you gather together some names, be sure to outline the scope of the work to be provided, how much you'll pay for this service, when you will pay, and any other specific items. Make sure the subcontractor answers your question, "What happens if you mess up?" to your satisfaction. For many service providers, the answer will be to limit their liability to what you've paid for the service. If this doesn't work for you, find someone else to employ.

Finally, and this goes for anyone you hire to do anything significant for you, spell out your agreement in writing. Be sure the contract specifies how much you will pay, what work is to be performed, and when. You and the service provider should both sign this document—handshake deals aren't worth much if you have to go to court. Keep a copy of the signed contract handy, In case a dispute arises.

Another source of information is your local home-improvement center. For the most part, the people who work at Home Depot, Lewes, Menards, and your local hardware store know quite a lot about the tools they sell and how best to use them. You might even find someone there who moonlights as a general handyman. For do-it-yourself information, Home Depot publishes a line of excellent books that take you through simple and complicated projects Step-by-Step.

Home Warranties

A home warranty, sometimes known as a *homeowner's warranty,* is like an extended service contract that you might buy when you purchase a used car. Its purpose is to give the buyer peace of mind that if something breaks down, the cost of the repair will be covered.

When home buyers purchase an existing home (also known as a "used" home), they worry that appliances and mechanical systems will break and be expensive to fix or replace. When you're spending every dime you have to purchase a home, the last thing you want to worry about is replacing the hot-water heater or an air-conditioner compressor or blower. Replacing a refrigerator could be $500 to $1,000; replacing a compressor could cost twice that.

So a few years ago, insurance companies came up with home warranty plans. The warranty guarantees that all mechanical systems (like the plumbing or electrical systems) and appliances (refrigerators, dishwashers, stoves, and so forth) that are working on the day of closing will continue to work for the first year someone owns your home. If something breaks, the new homeowner has a toll-free number to call. The company will send someone out to fix or replace the broken appliance or mechanical system. The homeowner pays a flat fee (which could be anywhere from around $50 to perhaps $150), and any costs above or beyond that are picked up by the company that issued the home warranty policy.

Home warranties are an excellent marketing tool because they provide a salve for the buyer's biggest worry—that something will go wrong in a house that isn't brand-new. Savvy sellers can use this as a marketing tactic. Purchasing one might reassure a nervous buyer that if something does go wrong, he or she has a place to turn (other than pursuing you, the seller, for cash to fix the problem). But they are also practical because they save the new homeowner time and money when it comes to finding someone to fix basic items in the house. The warranty company has repair contracts with local tradespeople. These are the same folks you would call, but that someone new to the neighborhood might not know.

The problem with home warranties is that the policies are somewhat expensive up front, and you have to pick a reliable and responsive warranty company, which means doing a little research. If you decide to purchase a home warranty, many real-estate agents sell them, or you can purchase one directly on the Web from a company like Countrywide Credit. (Countrywide Credit owns Countrywide Home Loans and also owns insurance and investing subsidiaries; go to www.countrywide.com.) American Home Shield (www.americanhomeshield.com) also sells homeowner's warranties online.

Buying a home warranty policy doesn't mean you don't have to fix things that are broken in your house. It is best used to make a home buyer feel protected in case something breaks *after* closing.

DON'T LIE ABOUT WHAT'S WRONG
WITH YOUR HOUSE

I don't know what homeowners are thinking when they lie about the true condition of their home. Well, that's not exactly true. I do know what they're thinking: No one is ever going to find out.

But, of course, with so many buyers using professional inspectors to scrutinize every nook and cranny of their future home, most problems will be uncovered. The ones that are missed can cause a much bigger problem down the line.

Consider this true story: A couple was looking to buy a home in the Los Angeles area. The husband and wife had purchased several homes over the years, in different locations, so they had some experience with buying and selling real estate. They had bought and sold several fixer-uppers, as well as several apartment buildings through the years.

They saw a house near Los Angeles, and thought it looked beautiful. But there were problems with the drainage in the garden. They asked the seller to fix the problem. When it came time to review the mandatory transfer disclosure statement the seller had signed, no major problems were indicated on the form. On top of that, the seller was a real-estate agent, well versed in the need for full and proper disclosure. And he worked for one of the biggest, most prestigious real-estate firms in southern California. Satisfied with the results of the disclosure, the buyers weren't too worried that something might be seriously wrong with the property.

They moved in. A short time later, the wife noticed water leaking from the first-floor ceiling. She also started having headaches and other strange aches and pains. Tearing out that one ceiling led to the startling discovery that the entire house was soaking from top to bottom on the inside. Tearing out plasterboard exposed mold that had been growing for a long time everywhere in the structure. And the one repair the buyers had asked the seller to make? The contractor who "fixed" the problem was told by the sellers to make it look like he did something, but not to do anything expensive. The cost of the "fix" was a few hundred dollars.

As we went to press, a legal case was wending its way through the court system. The house is a total loss. From breathing the mold-filled air, the wife claims that her brain function has been permanently damaged. And though the seller claimed he had "no idea" that there were water problems, letters surfaced from his tenants detailing the various problems they had had with water intrusion.

What was this seller thinking? It's difficult to know, and perhaps no one will ever find out. But it looks as though the seller has tried to defraud the buyers. It's true that the seller would have had a difficult, if not impossible, time unloading his moldy home for the same price he received from the buyers, but the damages assigned in a court case like this could completely ruin him, not to mention his reputation and livelihood.

What could this seller have done? He should have been honest from the beginning about the water-intrusion problems in the property. He could have sold the home as a teardown, that is, for its land value only. He should not have covered up the truth.

That's an extreme example, but it points to the simple truth: Lying doesn't pay in real estate. Home buyers get angry and sue, causing a tremendous amount of grief, anger, and expense. Listing agents often get dragged into the fray. Better to be honest up front.

My Home's Problems

Interior Problems   How Long?

_____

_____

_____

_____

_____

Exterior Problems   How Long?

_____

_____

_____

_____

A GOOD START

Does your home have any problems? Are there issues you wish weren't there? Using the list above, write down all the issues and problems your home has.

Once you've listed all the potential problems with your home, talk to an agent (perhaps the same agent who sold you the home) about what you can do to either cure the problem or make it less of an issue for buyers. For example, if you have a radon problem, you can probably eliminate the health hazard by introducing a system that airs out your basement. If you have a pest infestation problem, you may be able to fix it with common pest control methods.

If you don't know what problems lurk behind the walls in your home, consider having a professional home inspector do a prelisting inspection (for a detailed explanation, see Step 33). If you don't know what your state law says about seller disclosure, ask your agent (or check out Step 23 for details). But never lie. It will always come back to haunt you.

DON'T THINK YOU CAN FOOL THE HOME INSPECTOR

You may be able to fool some home buyers some or even all of the time, but you probably can't pull the wool over the eyes of a half-decent professional home inspector.

While these guys may miss something that's inside a wall (after all, they don't have X-ray vision), an inspector who's paying attention will notice things like a newly painted basement (could be hiding wet spots) or bubbling, flaking paint or paint discoloration in the ceiling (could be a leak).

Here are some things home sellers often do to try to fool home buyers:

- **Repainting basement walls and floors.** Unless your basement has been finished, there really isn't any reason to paint or repaint the basement walls just before listing your home. In fact, doing so may raise a red flag. The inspector might assume you're trying to hide flaws and will probably alert the home buyer to that possibility. Unfinished basement floors are almost never painted. If they are painted at all, or repainted just before closing, it's another red flag.

- **Heavy furniture or boxes pushed up against walls.** If the inspector can't move furniture or boxes in order to inspect a wall, a foundation, or a floor, that's cause for concern. Some sellers will stack immovable objects up against a floor to hide problems like cracks in the foundation, mold or moisture issues, and pest problems.

- **Rugs that can't be pulled up.** If you tack down a carpet or an area rug in the corners so it can't be lifted up, or if you object strenuously to a professional home inspector taking a peek below a carpet, you will raise a red flag. Unscrupulous sellers will often make it difficult for inspectors to do the job for which they're being paid.

- **Water valves that are shut off.** If you've got a water problem, shutting off the water valve isn't going to fool anyone. A good home inspector will turn on all the faucets in a home. If a faucet is broken, that will go into the inspector's report. Likewise, if it's warm out and the outdoor hoses aren't attached and working, the inspector is going to wonder why and will investigate.

- **Using pets as room guards.** In Chicago, a home seller didn't want the buyer (or broker, for that matter) to know he didn't have a basement. So he put a tape machine with a dog barking behind a closed and locked door. He told the broker it was for the broker's and buyers' safety. Once the home was sold, the buyer realized there was no basement, and a lawsuit ensued. Some home sellers use dogs and other pets to prevent buyers and brokers from entering rooms with problems. This isn't a long-term solution, since a savvy buyer will insist that the homeowner remove the animal so an inspector can get in to look at the room.

- **Repainting walls and ceilings.** If you have a water problem, painting over the problem area isn't a long-term solution. Many home inspectors carry moisture-sensitive equipment and can easily test walls and ceilings for moisture. If you have a synthetic stucco home and you know you have a moisture problem, repainting could seal in the moisture between the walls, causing even more long-term damage.

Scheming home sellers will find limitless ways to try to fool a home inspector, a broker, or a buyer. But this isn't the way to go.

A GOOD START

If you have a serious problem in your home that cannot be corrected without spending a great deal of time and money, you may want to deal with the problem by changing the way you market your home to the public. Although a home that is in top condition and looks fabulous will reap the top profit, it may not be worth your time to oversee a major renovation or project to correct a serious flaw.

If you have such a problem, talk to your agent. You might be able to develop a marketing strategy that will enable you to get as much money out of the property as possible. For example, selling "as is" might be one answer. You sell your home in "as is" condition, allowing for the possibility that there may be problems with your home that you don't know. By disclosing all known defects or problems up front, you discount the effect of any preclosing negotiation strategies your buyer may try. You might also present estimates from a couple of subcontractors on the cost and time involved in fixing the problem.

SIMPLE STEP

4

CHOOSE A BROKER WHO MATCHES YOUR HOME-SELLING TEMPERAMENT

What kind of seller are you? Years ago, I noticed that sellers typically fall into three basic categories:

- **Pie-in-the-sky sellers.** These individuals price their property higher than anything that's ever sold in their neighborhood and then wait to see if someone bites. Real-estate agents often have a difficult time with pie-in-the-sky sellers, who are completely unrealistic about how much their property is worth. Often, they price their home so far out of the ballpark that there is a real possibility the property will become stigmatized by the length of time it has been listed. On the other hand, when you have a hot sellers' market like the one that ran from 1995 through 2001, homes were selling for unbelievably high prices—prices so high, agents kept shaking their heads in disbelief. In this case, sellers that agents privately referred to as "pie in the sky" had a field day entertaining multiple offers in excess of the list price.

- **Realistic sellers.** These sellers do a thorough investigation of the market to find out how long it takes to sell a home like theirs and then price their home competitively. Agents prefer to work with realistic sellers because they understand market forces. In a hot sellers' market, realistic sellers will often field multiple bids because the competitive initial pricing of the property lets buyers know that this seller understands what his or her property is really worth.

- **Desperate and anxious sellers.** It's normal to have some concerns about selling your home. It's even normal to have a small anxiety attack from time to time. But there are sellers who are classic worriers, who spend an inordinate amount of time and energy thinking about every detail involved with a home sale and the amount of time it's taking to produce the right offer. If you need to move quickly, or if you feel you need to get a certain amount of cash from your sale, then you risk making a decision out of desperation rather than thinking things through objectively. The result of wearing your desperation on your sleeve? An unpleasant, stress-filled sales experience, and the possibility that you will net less cash than you otherwise might have.

Knowing what kind of seller you are will allow you to choose the right sort of agent. Just as there are different types of sellers, agents, too, have various temperaments. That means there are certain agents who will meet your needs better than others. There are two basic types of agents:

- **Laid-back agents.** These agents take a more relaxed approach: They may work part-time or full-time, and they may take plenty of vacations. In general, their style is to stay relaxed and get things done in a slower, perhaps more orderly way. As a seller, you may get more time and attention from an agent who works at a slightly slower pace, because he or she typically won't have as many clients as an aggressive agent.

- **Aggressive agents.** These agents are usually busy serving a variety of home buyers and sellers. They may be working with people buying or selling condos, town houses, and single-family homes, and with properties that are priced moderately and those that are at the very top of the local market. Aggressive agents frequently have assistants who prepare the paperwork and who may even do showings.

There are agents who chain-smoke and talk nonstop, and those who spend more time listening. Some agents eat only salads and drink black coffee, while others indulge in fast foods. There are agents who have small children, grown children, and no children at all. There are agents who are technologically savvy and use tools like e-mail and Internet-based scheduling software to stay in close communication with their clients, and there are agents who are tech-averse, for whom e-mail is difficult. There are young agents, just starting out their careers in the business, and those like my mother, Susanne, who have seen housing prices rise and fall during their twenty-plus years selling residential real estate.

In other words, there are agents to match every personality quirk a home seller could have. The trick is finding the right agent to match your temperament. Why?

Finding the right agent is like dating. Listing your property means a short-term "marriage" between you and your agent or broker. If you're not truly compatible with your agent, you won't be able to communicate effectively, and perhaps won't be able to stand each other. (Yes, it's true. Some agents hate their clients.) Either way, if the relationship isn't right, you'll have a hard time maxing out the profits in your home.

A GOOD START

Now is when you should start thinking about the type of seller you are. Take out paper and pencil (or use the worksheet on the following pages) and write down all the reasons you're selling your home. Your list might be short—perhaps you're selling because you've been transferred. Or perhaps you want to be in a better school district, or you want a better layout for entertaining, or you're having another child. Or perhaps you want to trade down because your children have grown and moved away. Your list should reflect all the reasons why you are selling your home today.

Why I Want to Sell

1. _____
2. _____
3. _____
4. _____
5. _____
6. _____
7. _____
8. _____

Next, decide how quickly you want to sell your home. Do you want to sell immediately, in three months, or perhaps in a year? The length of time you set aside to sell your home may dictate whether you're going to be more relaxed about your sale or anxious to get a move on. Check off the appropriate box.

How Quickly Do I Want to Move?

❏ 3 months or less
❏ 3 to 6 months
❏ 6 months to 1 year
❏ 1 to 2 years
❏ When my new house is finished
❏ When I retire

Finally, make a list of all the qualities you're looking for in an agent. Do you want him or her to be more aggressive or laid back? Do you want someone who smokes? Someone who is habitually on time and gets upset if you're late, or someone who is also running behind now and again?

What Qualities Do I Want in an Agent?

1. _____
2. _____
3. _____
4. _____
5. _____
6. _____
7. _____
8. _____

In Steps 36, 37, and 38, I'll discuss how to interview prospective agents to figure out which agent has the qualities you want and will make the best match for you. But if you don't do your homework and figure out what kind of a seller you are, you'll find it a lot harder to pick the right agent.

SIMPLE STEP

5

DON'T BE A PIG WHEN IT COMES TO MONEY

Pure, unadulterated greed is ugly.

Most of us are shocked and disgusted when we read news stories about big company officials enriching themselves at the expense of employees and shareholders. People who have hundreds of millions of dollars—more money than anyone would need in several lifetimes—selling out their ideals and principles in the name of the almighty greenback.

We've been conditioned from childhood to think that money doesn't matter, that it's a person's soul that counts. Most of us can't imagine selling our souls for any amount of money (though it's fun to watch movies that explore this very question).

But something interesting happens when it comes to selling our own homes. People who never quibble about who ordered what when dining out with friends suddenly become price-conscious when it comes time to list their property. They calculate over and over again how much cash they'll pocket from the sale of their home after expenses. They negotiate for every nickel and take a hard line on repairing or replacing items called to their attention in the home inspector's report. They're so focused on the bottom line, and how much they're walking away with, that the transaction becomes difficult for everyone involved.

For example, there are deals that die because the seller won't be flexible on the closing date. There are other deals that die because the seller won't do a minor repair or give a $200 credit because of the "principle" involved. There are sellers who do not negotiate simply because they were taken advantage of when they bought the home and feel it's now their turn to dish it out.

As I said, greed is ugly.

And yet, it's so easy to slip down the slope. It seems natural when negotiating to try to cut the best deal for yourself. So here's one of the great secrets of selling: The best deal you can make is one in which everyone walks away from the table happy.

My husband, Sam, and I used to live in a co-op apartment overlooking Lake Shore Drive in Chicago. It was an absolutely beautiful place, about two thousand square feet, with high ceilings, southern exposure, big rooms, and a six-burner stove in the kitchen. It had three bedrooms, three full bathrooms, and detailed moldings that dated from the 1920s, when the place was built. But when we tried to sell (about five years after we moved in), vintage co-ops weren't that popular. No one wanted to buy our apartment.

There were a couple of lowball bids we turned down. And one prospective buyer visited five times before deciding it wasn't quite right. And then, out of the blue, a buyer came through who seemed perfect. He made an offer for the apartment that was about 10 percent below our asking price. Sam and I decided this buyer was the one, and we immediately agreed to split the difference between what he offered and what we were asking. We felt lucky to get what we got, and he paid less than he anticipated. Everyone walked away from the table feeling good about the transaction, and that gave Sam and me a great deal of satisfaction on top of whatever money we made on that particular piece of real estate.

A GOOD START

How do you quell any feelings of greed you may have? One way is to take emotion out of your home sale. Sit down with your spouse or partner (or yourself, if you are the only owner of your property) and discuss what is the least amount of money you'd be happy getting for your home. This has nothing to do with the list price, but everything to do with the net amount you'd receive.

For example, let's say your home is listed for $225,000, but you know you'd be happy selling for $189,000. By knowing your minimum sales price, it gives you a way to keep a lid on any greedy feelings you may have. How? Because if a first offer comes in around or above $189,000, you know you'll hit or exceed your minimum sales price. Anything above that number is gravy.

While it's true that this is a little mind game you play with yourself, it really works because you're removing the element of gambling from the equation. There's no wondering how much higher someone will go, and no game to play, because you already know you'll be happy with whatever you get.

And in the long run, except in very special cases, an extra $500 or $1,000 isn't going to make that big a difference in your life. It may grease a few extra wheels, but it doesn't matter that much. What matters is that you were able to control the greed factor, which should enable you to sell your home faster and with fewer problems.

Nothing kills a deal faster than greed, and frequently agents remind sellers that their "first offer is the best offer." If the first offer exceeds your minimum sales price, that's great. You can negotiate in good faith. But if you get your first offer on the first day your home is listed, and it exceeds your minimum sales price, you may quickly wonder whether you've underpriced your home. Don't let the thought that you might be leaving money on the table get in the way of a successful negotiation. The proper response when you counter the offer is to stay a little closer to your list price. (Just make sure you do counter the offer, so that on the off chance the first offer is your right offer, you don't let it slip away.)

2

Cleaning House: Five Steps You Must Take Before You Sell

GET RID OF ALL THE CLUTTER

Ever noticed how quickly stuff collects on a clean countertop? In my house, stuff accumulates on our kitchen countertops like dust on a shelf. I suspect that's the case in your house, as well.

What ends up on a countertop? In my kitchen, you're likely to see mail from today, as well as opened envelopes and bills that arrived up to a week ago or longer, a manuscript for my next book that just came back from the publisher, the kids' art and school-work, notices sent home from school, lists, messages that contain important phone numbers, coupons, newspapers, magazines, the purse I'm currently using plus a smaller purse I used the night before, keys, games the kids were playing before school, and a collection of fruit ripening in a bowl.

When stuff starts falling off the countertop, we usually sort through it and put it away where it belongs. Stuff we can't figure out what to do with, or that we need to keep out of the kids' reach, ends up in another space, usually on top of the refrigerator.

Quite simply, people are collectors (or gatherers, if you're an anthropologist by nature), and so stuff just adds up. As kids, we bring home shells and stones, collect cars and fireflies, and have other assorted piles lying around our rooms. As adults, we become a bit more sophisticated in our choice of collections, but we have them all the same. (I know someone who has a collection of mini-motorcycles.) Even if your stuff is displayed beautifully, it has to go somewhere.

When you're selling your home, where you *don't* want it to go is on any horizontal surface. So, no piles of newspapers and magazines on the floor, no paperwork on the counters, no stacks of books stuffed messily into your bookcase, and no collection of boots, bags, and shoes thrown haphazardly onto the floor of your closet.

All these spaces should be cleaned so that prospective buyers have an easier time seeing what's really in your home. (You know, the stuff that'll be left behind once your belongings get packed onto the moving truck, like your walls, ceilings, floors, and closets!) If you make it more difficult for a prospective buyer to see the bones of your home, he or she will have to make a bigger mental leap in order to get to that magical place where first offers come from.

A GOOD START

There's no easy way to do this, so I advocate the tough-love policy of cleaning off countertops: **Take everything off the countertop, and wipe it clean with a paper towel or piece of cloth.**

This may seem a bit drastic, particularly in the kitchen. But it works.

In the Kitchen

In the kitchen, remove everything from your countertops, including cookbooks, pieces of paper, ripening fruits and vegetables, stirring implements next to the stove, hot pads, soap and sponges, and all small appliances. Now clean off the counter. Once you're done admiring how big and clean the countertop is, you can return three things (less if you have a smaller amount of space in which you work, more if you have a little extra room). Perhaps it will be the coffee grinder, the microwave, and the toaster oven. Or perhaps it will be the coffeepot, an attractive container of slotted spoons, and a vase of flowers. Or perhaps something else.

Remember this: Whatever goes on top of any countertop should be attractive, artfully arranged, and sparklingly clean.

In the Bathrooms

Remove toothbrushes, hand towels, and soap. Clean the countertop, and then place an attractive soap dispenser (or a small dish with colored soaps) on the counter.

In the Living Room and the Dining Room

Remove all objects from the tabletops except, perhaps, the occasional vase of fresh, dried, or pretty silk flowers and plants, or a nice arrangement of coffee-table books. If you have a bookshelf and display knickknacks or objects d'art, arrange the objects so that there is a lot of "white" (or open) space around each piece. This might mean putting a few items away in a box until you move. That will allow the buyer's eye to rest and encourage him or her to experience the space as attractive but not overly cluttered.

If it's January 1, or any day thereafter, and you still have holiday cards displayed in your family room or living room, fold them up and remove them. If you're selling your home, you should remove any holiday displays no later than the first week of January. We'll talk more about holiday decorations and what to do with them in Step 32.

Other Horizontal Surfaces

On any other horizontal surface, be sure to take everything off and only put a few things back. The exception to this rule is your closet floor. If you don't have a proper shoe rack, you might want to buy one to organize your closet floor. If not, neatly line up your shoes and boots. But if you can find a way to get your shoes off the floor, that's a better solution. Finally, find a way to hang your purses and belts.

What should you do with everything you've removed from your countertops? If you can't find an attractive place to display the items, throw them away, give them away, or pack them away. Whether you decide to throw, give, or pack away these objects, you'll be miles ahead of the game when it comes time to move.

The Clutter Collector

One of the big parts of cleaning is organizing. By now, your home should be clutter free. If you find it's impossible to keep stuff from collecting, purchase a large flat storage box (it can be plastic or cardboard, but should be sturdy yet light to carry). This will be your clutter collector.

Keep this box in the place where your clutter collects, either in the kitchen or the dining room or wherever the mail is dropped off. When mail comes in, or paperwork from the kids' schools, or whatever, put it in this box. You might find receipts, old phone messages, stray change, pens and pencils, your kids' artwork from school, permission slips for school trips, and the like. Make this box the center repository for all household clutter.

When it comes time for a showing, simply take the box and slide it under a bed. After the showing, the box can come out again. While prospective buyers might look under the bed, all they would see is a simple, clean box filled with miscellaneous items. But home buyers typically don't look under beds during a first showing. In the ten to twenty minutes they've allotted to viewing your home, the only thing they're interested in is deciding how well the amenities of your home meet their own wants and needs, and whether it is worth coming back a second time. The contents of the box under your bed will be of no interest.

But what happens when a home buyer comes back for a second showing? You can take your clutter collector and move it elsewhere (though I've always found the under-the-bed trick works beautifully).

Just remember, having the clutter collector doesn't free you of the responsibility of actually going through those papers and making a decision about what to do with them. It just gives you an easy out for keeping your home clutter free during showings. (For a guide to which personal papers you need to keep and what stuff can be thrown away, take a look at one of my financial books, such as *50 Simple Things You Can Do to Improve Your Personal Finances*.)

SIMPLE STEP

7

PAINT YOUR INTERIORS WHITE

Real-estate agents know that homes that are light and bright sell faster and for more money than dark, dreary homes. Gloomy homes might have windows facing north, or walls that are papered or painted in dark colors or with heavy patterns. Light, bright homes feel bigger to buyers than do darker homes, and space is, next to location, the primary consideration.

How do you make a home light and bright? The solutions are easy:

- Draw back your curtains.

- Change window treatments. Exchange heavy draperies for white vinyl miniblinds.

- Paint your home a light, neutral color, or even brilliant white.

- Increase the wattage of the lightbulbs in your fixtures. (Be sure you don't exceed the recommended wattage for each fixture, or your fixture could melt or turn into a fire hazard.)

Paint Colors

Why paint your home in neutrals or white? Artists and designers will tell you that light colors reflect light. Dark colors tend to absorb it. So if you paint your dining room some shade of dark red, the room will look much smaller than if the walls are painted eggshell with white trim in high gloss. (Remember, you're playing to the buyer's expectations of getting as much space as possible for the money.)

Neutral colors, including white, help buyers think of your home as a blank canvas. For some reason, it's easier to imagine how your stuff will look in someone else's house if the walls are neutral and there aren't too many distractions like artwork, kids' posters, photos, wall hangings, framed degrees, bulletin boards, and other vertical decorations. Also, almost everyone has lived in a room with white walls at some point, like in a dorm room at college. White may be a little stark, but it feels familiar and goes with almost any décor.

Painting Adds to Your Profit

If you need another reason to repaint, consider this: In every survey conducted on the topic, painting your home white or a neutral color returns several times the amount of the investment. For example, if it costs you $1,500 to repaint your home white, you might be able to get as much as $5,000 back in additional profit! (And with painting, you can do much, if not all, of the work yourself, limiting your investment to time and materials.)

A GOOD START

If you haven't repainted the interior of your home in several years, consider painting the whole thing a couple of weeks before you sell your home. Even if you have to hire someone, that fresh coat of paint will make your home stand out from the crowd.

Once you've made the decision about how much to paint, you have to determine what colors will work best. I personally think pure white paint is the way to go, but some people prefer neutrals like eggshell, off-white, or even light gray. If you have trim around your windows and doors, consider painting that some sort of semigloss white to give a fresh, crisp look to whatever color you put on your walls.

If you have wallpaper that isn't in great shape, consider peeling off the paper and repainting the room. Even if you choose a dark color with white trim, the effect will be better than to have unsightly, bubbling, or peeling wallpaper.

Most paint stores have the ability to match the color of any paint chip or color sample you provide. If you want to find the exact color of mocha latte to match a stripe on your sofa, you probably can do it. Any decent home supply store should have a person on staff who can assist you with finding the right color shades. When choosing your paint colors, remember that light, bright, and neutral can help pump up your profits.

CLEAN OR REPLACE YOUR
CARPET AND FLOORS

When my friends Ellen and Michael bought their condo, their agent told them they'd have to replace their floors someday. "There wasn't enough wood left to do another sanding," said the agent, who also noted that over the years the original wood floors had warped and cracked.

Wood floors can take a beating from the weather. Indoor humidity and extreme temperature changes can cause floors to separate, and moving around heavy furniture will scratch even hardwood floors. Accidents with water, from bursting pipes to large spills, can do damage, as well. If you're buying a home with hardwood floors, you want them to be in good shape. Unsightly or damaged hardwood can cause a home buyer to walk out the door.

But the condition of other types of floors and rugs can cause problems for home buyers, as well. Cleaning, changing, or improving these floor coverings can increase your ultimate profit.

When Max was going to sell his home, one of the first things he did was pull up the entry hallway and bathroom tile floor and replace it with new vinyl tile from the local home-improvement center. Then he replaced the awful, dated rug with relatively inexpensive off-the-rack, off-white carpeting from Home Depot. Those two changes, plus replacing a few broken window sashes, helped Max net nearly $30,000 in extra profit when he sold his home later that year. He spent just $5,000 on the improvements, including the carpet.

The bottom line is this: Home buyers perceive surfaces to be extremely important. Whether it's the walls, the ceilings, or the floors, if these are in great condition, the buyer will probably assume that the rest of the home is in good condition, as well. (Of course, this may not be true, but at least the home will look polished.)

When Emanuele and Gerhard starting looking for another home to buy, they were immediately taken with a fabulous 1920s vintage apartment near downtown Chicago. What did they like about the condo? "Every wall was perfectly smooth and every floor was finished perfectly," Emanuele told me. While the kitchen would need to be redone, "you felt like you could move right in." Which is what every buyer wants.

A GOOD START

Stand in the front doorway of your home and look down at the floors.

- Is the hardwood cracked, separating, badly scratched, or dinged?
- Are there ceramic or marble tiles that have cracked or chipped?
- Is the vinyl floor buckling?
- Are the vinyl tiles peeling in the corners?
- Is the carpet filthy? Can it be saved with a professional shampooing? Or will it have to be replaced?

Now go into each room of the house and ask yourself the following question: How much better would this room look if the floor coverings were cleaned or replaced?

Don't limit your inspection to floors and tile. In the bathrooms it's also important that any area rugs or bath mats be scrutinized. Because the use of hot water increases the humidity in most bathrooms, area rugs, floor towels, or bath mats can begin to smell of mildew (or mold, if you really let things go). Consider replacing the bath mat or rug to keep the room looking and smelling fresh. (And if the situation calls for an entire new set of towels for display, well, that's probably also a good investment that you'll enjoy in your next home, as well. See Step 13 for more tips.) If your unfinished basement floor is looking spotty or dirty, wash it well. If that part of the basement seems dark, consider painting the floor to spruce it up. (If you decide to paint the basement floor, remember that an inspector might see it as a red flag.)

Always consider how a thorough, professional steam cleaning will make your floors and carpets look before you decide to replace them. When it comes to ceramic tile, your local home-improvement store ought to have tubes of ointments that can lighten your grout. If you have to replace your carpet, choose a neutral color that will go with almost any type of decor. Avoid buying pure white or very light off-white rugs. Although the color will look fantastic the first day, it's difficult to keep clean, especially if you have young children or pets, and particularly during showings. (Having an open house on a rainy or snowy day can be torture with a pure white rug. If you go that route, you could find yourself cleaning the carpet several times over before you sell your home.)

You should also choose something practical. White tile is beautiful in a bathroom, but the tile and white grout can be difficult to keep clean. If you buy beige tile, and use beige grout, it will be easier to keep clean while you're selling your home. Check your local yellow pages for discount tile outlet centers where you can buy designer tile on sale, or check your local home-improvement store.

Resources

If you're so inclined, installing ceramic tile can be done cheaply and easily. Your local bookstore or home-improvement center should have books that demonstrate how to do this. The Sunset line of home-improvement books is good, as are the Home Depot line of fixer-upper books. I also like the Black & Decker and Reader's Digest home-improvement titles. The best selection of these titles is usually available at your home-improvement store, not at a bookstore.

The additional benefit of buying the books at your home-improvement store is that someone is on staff who can help you buy the tools and supplies you need for a particular job, saving you another trip.

TURN ON YOUR LIGHTS DURING SHOWINGS

If, as real-estate agents say, homes that are light and bright show better and sell for more money, what's the point in leaving the lights off? All you're doing is giving the buyer the wrong first impression of your home. Once you do that, you're fighting an uphill battle to get the buyer to change his or her mind.

When I bought my co-op, back in 1989, the room that was to become my office was really dark. It had red, black, and white plaid wallpaper, which was also on the bathroom walls. The floor had a red and black shag carpet. The windows were covered with blackout shades in the same pattern, and there were shutters (always closed during showings) over every window to block out any other light that might come in. (Of course, these windows overlooked a beautiful synagogue and Lake Michigan, nothing you'd ever want to see!) Plus, none of the lights were on in the apartment when we went in to see it.

As my late stepfather, Leon, would later say, "You've got to have a pretty good imagination to have bought this place."

When my sister, Phyllis, looked at the house she would eventually buy, the shutters in the master bedroom were closed. When she opened them to see what the windows and the view looked like, she found huge cobwebs strung from every corner. She also discovered broken windows, dust balls, filthy windows, and even garbage.

Most home buyers don't have the time or inclination to indulge their imagination and think about all the wonderful things they could do to your home. And some people have no talent for decorating. People seeking fixer-uppers will immediately recognize the opportunity a property in this kind of condition represents, but that's just a fraction of the total buying population. Most folks simply want to purchase a home that's light and bright and ready to move into on the day they close.

If you want them to see the light, turn on your lights!

A GOOD START

If you want buyers to be satisfied that your house is light and bright enough for them, you have a few choices:

- **Turn on all the lights in your home.** That includes lights in the closets, stairs, basement undercabinet lights, and bathrooms.
- **Buy additional light fixtures.** Table lamps with 100- to 150-watt bulbs will help. Ceiling fixtures with 100- to 150-watt halogen lights will add natural-type light. Inexpensive but attractive fixtures can be bought at your local home-improvement stores, or stores like Costco, The Great Indoors, Target, and EXPO.
- **Increase the wattage in your existing fixtures.** But be careful not to put in bulbs that exceed the recommended wattage or you could end up with melting fixtures and a fire hazard.

Let's go over these options in greater detail.

One of the biggest problems sellers have are dark spots in a house. Typically, rooms like the basement, tucked-away storage closets, garages, and bedroom closets are poorly lit.

Even if you turned on the one bare bulb hanging from the ceiling, it probably wouldn't be enough to make a difference.

One easy fix is to simply replace all the burned-out light-bulbs in your home. (You'd be surprised how many homes have at least one or two missing lightbulbs. Look for fixtures that have two lightbulbs but seem dim—undoubtedly you'll find that one of the two bulbs is out.) This should be done well before you invite agents in to do their comparative marketing analysis (see Step 36 for information on CMAs), and you should stay on lightbulb patrol until you and the buyer have come to terms.

You should also consider upgrading your low-watt light fixtures to provide brighter overhead lighting. You can purchase inexpensive but stylish fixtures at any of the home-improvement stores I've already mentioned, or even through the Internet at places like Crate & Barrel and Pottery Barn. Buy fixtures that give you at least 100 watts for a closet and up to 240 watts for each bedroom. I'm a big fan of halogen lighting, which more closely mirrors natural daylight. A 100-watt halogen bulb might appear give off as much light as 200 watts of incandescent light. The bulbs are more expensive, but they could add a neat finishing touch to a room, while also brightening it up. And if you buy a "torchiere" halogen lamp, you can take it with you to your new home. (Make sure you purchase a good-quality halogen lamp and keep it away from your curtains.)

How much is too much light? I like light, so I'm not sure you can ever have too much of it in a home. I think it's better to go overboard and overwhelm a buyer with a bright home than let anyone feel it may be too dark.

If you have a spot in a room that needs additional lighting, consider buying an attractive tabletop lamp. Also, take a look at your lampshades. It could be that they're filthy, tattered, or perhaps dark or heavily patterned. (Remember, dark colors absorb light.) Consider replacing them with new light shades.

If you're worried about running up the electricity bill during the home sale process, don't be. This is part of the cost of selling your home. In fact, don't even think about it.

Before you leave your home before a showing, turn on all the lights in the house. If, as is common in many parts of the country, the seller's agent doesn't turn up at a showing and the buyer and the buyer's agent are left to walk through your home unescorted, it's better to have all the lights on than have the buyer stand around twiddling his or her thumbs while the agent tries to find your light switches. Or worse, you could wind up with a buyer whose agent turns on only a couple of lights and shows a dark house to a prospective buyer!

(If you're selling during the summer, you should also leave your air conditioner on to keep your home cool. If you're selling during winter, you should leave your heat on to make your home more comfortable. If you're showing during the summer, your home should never be warmer than 74 degrees. If you're showing during the winter, it should never be cooler than 69 degrees.)

Don't leave a note asking the agent to turn off the lights when he or she leaves. Although that may seem polite, you may have more than one showing in a day, and you'll want your home looking as bright as it can from the first showing until the last.

CREATE A NO-DUST ZONE

I once went to an open house in Boston. The neighborhood was filled with charming, turn-of-the-century brownstones and three-family row houses. The one- and two-bedroom condominiums I saw were perfect starter homes, and all were in about the same physical condition. But one of the homes was so filthy that the real-estate agent (who at the time worked for the seller) apologized profusely for the poor condition of the home.

"Well, of course he isn't expecting to get the list price," she said offhandedly, breaking a bunch of real-estate ethics and laws in one fell swoop.

The dirty secret about some people is that they live like pigs. Just about every agent can recall at least one seller or more who left beds unmade, dirty underwear and socks strewn around the bedroom and the bathroom, and a sink full of dishes with several days' food caked on them.

More commonly, sellers simply fail to clean—dust balls the size of basketballs roll around behind couches, and their smaller cousins collect under chairs. You find sofas with sticky goo from leaky kids' cups, chairs with stained fabric, and carpets so stained they look a different color entirely.

Even if you do your own basic housekeeping, or hire someone to come in and do it for you, your house or condo probably won't be clean enough for a showing. Showing your home requires a top-to-bottom cleaning that sheds light into every dark corner and freshens up the dankest of closets. Mix Martha Stewart with Mr. Clean, and you'll begin to get an idea of what I'm talking about.

Why is cleanliness so important? Believe it or not, "clean" appeals to home buyers. And nothing keeps away buyers better than a dirty, smelly home. Although most home buyers will do their own cleaning once they close on your home, vigilant cleaning is part of the overall maintenance of a home. It shows that you've taken care of it and makes buyers think you've probably taken care of all the other regular maintenance, as well.

So make cleaning your home a priority. Once the first major cleaning is done, do a thorough follow-up at least once a week while your home is on the market (more often if you have small children). Then pick up and do a quick dusting just before a showing. I've found a little Pledge and Windex also give a room a nice clean smell, reinforcing the "clean, clean, clean" image you're trying to project.

A GOOD START

The supplies you need to really scrub your home are nominal: some sort of cleaning spray (Fantastic, 409, and other all-purpose cleaners); a window cleaner (like Windex); Murphy's Oil Soap for wood floors (if you have a wax finish); white vinegar; and a bath, tub, and tile cleaner (like Soft Scrub). Your tools should include sponges, a mop, a broom, a couple of kitchen towels, and a few rolls of paper towels. I also find it helpful to keep some of those disinfectant wipes handy, like the Clorox wipes. They're particularly useful in bathrooms, especially if you have young children.

Start at one end of your home and work to the other. Don't forget to sweep in the corners and under each piece of furniture. Wash the windows inside and out, if possible; if not, consider hiring a window-cleaning company. Clean your bathroom mirrors, and, if weather permits, sweep out your outdoor porch or terrace. Pay special attention to your kitchen and bathrooms, since home buyers are likely to focus their attention there.

Don't forget the basement, the attic, and the garage, which should also be spotless. Sam and I once looked at a hundred-year-old home. The basement was so clean you could have eaten off it. Fifteen years after we last saw that home, we still talk about how clean the basement was. It made quite an impression, even though we didn't buy the house. (Why not? It wasn't the condition, which was impeccable. We didn't really care for the location, and the house's one bathroom was on the second floor.)

In the Kitchen

Nothing turns off a home buyer faster than a dirty kitchen. And that's the conundrum: Kitchens are notoriously difficult to keep clean because we use them so frequently. When selling your home, work to keep your kitchen spotless so that dirt and grime don't build up.

Before a showing, wash the floors, clean the countertops and the stove, and make sure there are no sticky fingerprints on the refrigerator handle. If you keep your kids' photos and artwork, or an eccentric magnet collection on your refrigerator, consider removing these items until after you've sold.

Clean out the inside of your refrigerator once a week, and be sure to throw out any old, moldy, or smelly food. In our house, we stick to the seven-day rule: If food in open containers or leftover food hasn't been eaten in seven days, it goes out. With milk, if it goes a day or so beyond the expiration date, it goes out, as well. Be sure to put a new box of baking soda in your refrigerator and freezer to help contain odors. Keep a lid on overstocking during your selling season, because buyers like to feel as though the refrigerator will be big enough for their family. This is true even if you live in a location where it's common to take the refrigerator when you sell.

If you like to cook pungent foods, such as Indian, Asian, or Latin American dishes, you may find your kitchen retains the faint aroma of these dishes. No matter how often you clean your kitchen, you may find it difficult to remove those odors. If that's the case, you may end up simply repainting the kitchen to remove the smells, and avoid cooking these foods until after you've sold your home. (If you cook these foods frequently, but don't think your kitchen has retained any odors, ask a friend to drop by for a "sniff test." Our sense of smell can be dulled over time, and a fresh, objective nose might be of help.)

In the Bathrooms

Home buyers always take a close look at the bathrooms in a home, even on a first showing. Find the spots where dirt and grime collect in your bathroom. If you have a lot of little boys running around, it could at the base of the toilet. If you have babies, you may have a bathtub full of toys. If you have teenage girls, their bathroom could easily overflow with various tubes, pots, and containers of makeup.

Before each showing, wipe down your toilet and sink with a little Windex or Fantastic, or use one of the Clorox wipes. (If you don't have small children, try keeping a tub of them under each sink or in the medicine cabinet.) If the floor has hair or is dirty, be sure to wipe it up. Don't forget to wipe down any spotty faucets.

Wood-Burning Fireplace

If you have a wood-burning fireplace and use it frequently, be sure to sweep out the ashes before each showing, and either leave it empty or lay down a nice log display. And since ash tends to filter out into the room, be sure to spend a little extra time dusting to get rid of any soot.

The same holds true if you light a lot of candles. Burning candles can throw a fair amount of soot into the air, which tends to settle in the strangest places, like on ceilings, windows, halls, mirrors, and your artwork. If you use candles and like to display them, make sure they look attractive, and that you keep the wicks trimmed.

Children's Spaces

I took a short break when rewriting this section of the book to clean up our basement again. Sam and I have found that when you have young children (ten years of age or younger), it's difficult to keep their rooms and play spaces clean unless you have help all day, every day (which, like most of America, we don't).

In our basement this morning, we found tiny beads everywhere (the boys had been stringing necklaces with some of their friends earlier in the week and—surprise, surprise—one of the bowls tipped over), along with the colored pegs of the Lite Bright set, two sets of Tinkertoys, DVDs that hadn't been put back in their cases, CD-ROM games, more crayons and washable markers than I even knew we had, the pieces of a Hot Wheels set that had come apart, and magnetic little doodads that go into a box with a magnetic blackboard to generate creative intelligence, or whatever it's supposed to do. There were squishy balls, a Nerf football, round pegs, and puzzle pieces. We even found the missing piece of a puzzle game we had donated to the boys' school a year earlier! (Miss Ann will be happy about that.)

After an hour of putting away all the little pieces, including separating two distinct sets of Candyland pieces, we were able to finally vacuum the basement and organize the toy closet. All of which reminded me how difficult it is to keep little children and their toys organized. But when you're selling, succumbing to the mess isn't an option.

With older children, you can try to give them certain incentives to keep their rooms and play spaces clean. (Okay, we're talking bribes, but whatever works in your family.) I've found that withholding something the child values (television, movies, play dates, sleepovers, dessert, and so on) works better than rewarding the child with new toys, games, and dolls, which will just mean more stuff for you to help keep clean and organized. Younger children can keep some things neat, but their idea of organization won't mesh with the kind of Zen organization you need for successfully selling your home. Then again, every little bit helps.

Start small: Ask your children to put their dirty clothes in the hamper and their books back on the bookshelf. That can lead to making the bed, hanging up their towels in the bathroom, and other sorts of easy tasks. Even if they do only these small things when they're young, it will mean a little less work for you.

3

Spaces You See: Bedrooms, Bathrooms, Kitchen, Living Room, Dining Room, Family Room, and Home Office

DO MINOR REMODELS, NOT MAJOR RENOVATIONS, BEFORE YOU SELL

Before you sell your home, you'll have to fight the temptation to fix everything that's wrong with it. But gutting your home before you sell isn't practical—either emotionally or financially.

From the broken hinge on the bedroom door to the hanging shelf in the coat closet downstairs to the cracked grout between the bathroom tiles, there are a host of small, inexpensive remodeling projects you can do that will help you sell your home more quickly, and probably for more money.

What you don't want to do is tackle a major renovation or rehab project that could cost you thousands of dollars, mess up your home, and delay your projected list date. According to one study, most major remodeling projects, like gutting your kitchen or bathrooms, will not pay back the amount of money you spend on them—if you have to sell within a year of completion.

And that amount doesn't take into account the mess, aggravation, and time you've put into finding the right contractors, choosing the right appliances and finishes, and working through all of the problems that come up during a major renovation.

A GOOD START

When selling your home, concentrate on the minor remodeling project, not the major renovation. Start by creating two lists: A "must-do" list and your "wish" list for minor jobs.

Your must-do list should include the following:

- Any projects you started that are now partially complete.
- Any projects that will improve your home aesthetically.
- Any project that if left undone has the potential to derail your home sale.

Everything else you've always wanted to do but never got around to doing should go on your wish list (which I'll get to in a moment).

While your must-do list would seem to include everything, the fact is that you've limited yourself to the essential items that will increase your odds of selling at the price you want. Still, depending on the condition of your home, the list could be lengthy.

To create the list, grab a notebook and pen (or photocopy the worksheet below) and walk through your home as if you were a prospective buyer on a showing.

Start by standing on the sidewalk outside of your house or town house. Scrutinize every nook and cranny of the exterior. Is the paint cracked either on the siding or around the windows? Are the window lintels (the support beam or row of bricks or concrete that support the windows) failing? Do your home's windows need washing? Do the screens or storms need repairing? Does the brick need tuck pointing (a process whereby the chinks in the mortar are filled and repaired)? Is the driveway pavement faded and in need of blacktopping?

Walk into your home. Is the interior in perfect condition? What would it take to get it into the best shape possible, excluding a major renovation? For example, could your walls use a fresh coat of white paint? Carpet cleaning? Regrouting bathroom or kitchen tiles?

Must-Do Home-Improvement List

1. _____
2. _____
3. _____
4. _____
5. _____
6. _____
7. _____
8. _____
9. _____
10. _____
11. _____
12. _____

You're looking for reasons a buyer would choose not to purchase your home. For many buyers, the cost of painting and thoroughly cleaning a home can be reason enough not to make an offer.

If you never replaced the glass on a broken light fixture, now is the time to do it. Or purchase a new, inexpensive light fixture from your local home-improvement store. Do the ceiling fans and the kitchen appliances work? Do you have any broken storm windows or torn screens that need replacing or fixing before you list your home?

Once you take care of the must-do list, you can decide what, if anything, on your wish list you should tackle. Again, the point of doing a wish-list home-improvement or remodeling job, which could be much more time consuming and expensive to complete, is to increase the amount of cash you walk away with at the closing.

Home-Improvement Wish List

1. _____
2. _____
3. _____
4. _____
5. _____
6. _____
7. _____
8. _____
9. _____
10. _____
11. _____
12. _____

If putting down a new tile floor in the kitchen will cost you $300, but your agent says you can raise your list price by $1,000, that's a project you should probably complete before you list your home. Even if you can't increase your list price, you should do the project if your agent tells you the condition of the floor may discourage buyers from making an offer.

One of the best ways to prioritize your must-do and wish lists is to visit other homes that are similar to yours that are for sale in your neighborhood. Take advantage of weekend and weeknight open houses to walk through and see what amenities these homes offer and what condition they are in. You'll find them listed in your local paper's real-estate section or by driving around looking for "Open House" signs on the weekend.

Then go back home and reexamine your must-do and wish lists. If necessary, reprioritize your lists based on how much time you have and how your home compares to those already on the market.

EDIT YOUR FURNISHINGS

Some people are born with the eye: the ability to purchase and arrange furniture, art, and knickknacks in a way that makes their home look as though it were designed by a high-priced interior designer. My friends Gerhard and Emanuele have this natural talent. Whenever I walk through their front door, I feel as though I'm walking onto the pages of *Metropolitan Home* magazine. And nothing ever stays in the same place. Furniture is constantly being moved from room to room, or even shifted from wall to wall within the same room. No matter where each piece of furniture ends up or what gets added into the mix, the house still looks perfect.

While you may never achieve this level of style, you can still develop a talent for making your home look like a showpiece when you sell. By developing this ability, you'll be able to make your home stand out from the crowd. And by standing out, you'll be much more likely to draw a better offer than your competition.

The most important thing to do is to "edit" your furnishings. In this use, *edit* is a high-priced designer word that essentially means "less is more." By the time we go to sell our home, most rooms are overstuffed. As I've noted earlier, we have so many things in each room, or hanging on each wall, that the buyer's eye never gets a chance to rest. So, he or she ends up feeling exhausted, distracted, or perhaps even a bit overwhelmed by the decor and may not connect with the bones of your home.

When you edit your furnishings, what you're doing is helping the buyer imagine how his or her own furniture, art, and other stuff will look in your home. (It's the same reason I suggest you paint your home white or in neutral tones. This trick makes it easier for buyers to imagine their own stuff in your home—just give them a white or canvas background.)

When you remove furniture from a room, or paintings from a wall, or pieces from an étagère, or books from a bookcase or cabinet, what you're doing is creating "white space." You're emptying the air around that object so that it has more space to itself. The effect is to magnify the space in a room, so your room looks bigger. (The roominess is intensified with white paint.)

You'll fool the buyer's eye into seeing more space in a room than there really is. If you're worried that this is unethical, don't be. You're not changing the shape or proportion of a particular room, and you're not claiming on the listing sheet that the room has bigger dimensions. What you're doing is showing the buyer how to make the most of a particular space.

A GOOD START

When you were cleaning off your countertops, I suggested that the best way to do this is the tough-love approach: Remove everything, and then add back a few necessary and attractive items. Well, a similar approach works well when it comes to editing your furniture, art, and other items in a room.

Look around at each room in your home. Ask yourself the following questions:

1. **Is this room overcrowded?** Do I feel tired just looking at it?

2. **Can I remove one piece of furniture from this room?** If I do that, which piece will have the biggest

impact? (In a living room, removing the sofa might have the biggest impact, but most buyers have a sofa that they'll want to go into a living room, so it's probably best to remove a chair or end table and let the buyers think their sofa will fit in your living room.)

3. **How can I rearrange the furniture that's left in this room so that the room feels bigger?** Moving the sofa from one wall to another, or even into the middle of the room—depending on the size and shape of your room—can make a huge difference. When trying to create additional space in her 1,200-square-foot apartment, my mother-in-law, Marilyn, moved her sofa from the middle of the living room 3 feet back so that it rested against the wall. Moving the sofa those 3 feet opened up the entire room and not only made it feel much bigger, but made it much easier to move around (particularly for all the small grandchildren who visit).

4. **Do I have enough white space around each work of art hanging on the wall?** A good rule of thumb is to place only one good-size piece of art (or wall hanging or other wall-mounted object) per wall in a normal-size room. If you have a particularly long wall or hallway, try to limit the number of pieces of wall art to just a few.

5. **Do I have too many plants in this room?** Don't turn your living room or dining room into a greenhouse. One large plant or tree (and it should be a thriving, well-proportioned one) is enough for any room unless you have a conservatory attached to it.

Once you've answered these questions, you can start removing pieces of furniture from your room and artwork from your walls. If you can store them unobtrusively in your basement or in a closet, fine. But if that starts mucking up those spaces, consider renting a storage locker for the next few months until you sell your home. You can check out local storage lockers in the phone book. When you visit them, be sure to look at what kind of security, ventilation, hours, prices, and access they offer.

After you've completed the editing process, walk through your home again to see if it feels more spacious to you. If you can't answer yes to that question, start the editing process all over again.

If It Still Doesn't Feel Right . . .

If you don't know how to edit, pick up a couple of home decorating magazines, particularly ones that feature a more modern or stark look (like *Metropolitan Home* magazine or even *Martha Stewart Living*). Page through the magazines and pay close attention to how many paintings are on the walls and how much furniture is in each room. You'll notice that the rooms that look the biggest typically have the fewest things in them.

REDECORATE IN SMALL, SIMPLE WAYS, IF NECESSARY

Recently, I was having a conversation with Rick, the managing broker of a successful real-estate company in downtown Chicago, about various homes listed for sale and how they were decorated. I told him about some truly ugly homes I had seen and asked him what he tells homeowners who ask him how they can improve their home and the price they can get.

"Well, you know, Ilyce," he said slowly. "All homeowners think they have good taste." And then he told me that whatever suggestions he makes, he does so very carefully, so as not to hurt the homeowner's feelings.

The problem is that not every homeowner has good taste, and to pretend otherwise can be a nightmare for an agent trying to help that person pump up the potential profit.

Luckily, fixing up your home for sale doesn't mean you have to gut it and replace all of your furnishings. Very often, what's required is a little editing (as discussed in Step 12), and the purchase of a few key items that can give a whole new look to the different rooms of your home. This concept is known as "staging," and there are professionals who, for a fee, will "stage" your home so that it looks perfect for sale. (Some stagers will even empty your home and rent furniture that shows off a home's best features.)

For example, buying a new set of matching towels for the bathroom will dramatically add to the "finished" look of the room.

You can replace gunked-up soap dispensers with attractive colored soaps in a small pewter or stone holder or a container of colored liquid soap. You can buy a new toothbrush holder that matches the cup holder and other items in a bathroom.

A new bedspread, comforter cover, and pillows can give a fresh look to your bedroom. New, matching lampshades can make the nightstands look balanced even if the lamp bases are different. A small area rug can add color even if you put it over the regular carpet.

When each room of your home is done in a different color scheme and feel, it can make a less-sophisticated home buyer uncomfortable. By adding small touches in the right places, you have the opportunity to unify your house thematically, which will make it more appealing for the buyer.

A GOOD START

Walk into your living room and take a look around. Does anything catch your eye?

Each room in your home should have a focal point that will draw a buyer's eye. If you have windows with a fabulous view, you might want to hang a minimal set of curtains (perhaps something light or sheer) to encourage buyers to walk toward the view (and don't forget to keep them open during showings, even if the curtain material is sheer). If you have a huge wood-burning fireplace, you may want to show that off with a decorative piece of art, a spotlight in the ceiling, or an attractive noncombustible display in the hearth. (If you don't use the fireplace, but it works, you may want to clean it out and lay down fresh logs so it looks as though you could light it at any moment.) What you don't want to do is what one homeowner did: paint a working fireplace black and put plastic plants in the hearth.

Once you decide what each room's focal point should be, you need to edit the furnishings in the room so that nothing detracts from that object or piece of furniture. Next, you need to meet your buyer's expectations that each room can be a "set piece" on its own. By this, I mean each room should look completely put together.

Each bathroom should have its own set of matching towels hanging from a nice towel bar, beautiful little soaps (or an attractive container of liquid soap) with matching little pots holding things like Q-tips, cotton balls, razors, and other bathroom necessities. Place attractive, matching hand towels in the powder room along with a small vase of fresh flowers (if your sink has room) before each showing. Buy a new clear plastic liner for your shower curtain (or perhaps a new white shower curtain, too). If you have clear shower doors, make sure they sparkle.

Each bedroom should have a fresh bedspread or comforter cover with matching throw pillows. If you have a couch or chair in the room, consider adding a pillow or throw that matches the colors on the bed. Consider carrying the theme over toward matching curtains that hang from an attractive rod. Nightstands should be matching or in some way balance each other, and they should have either matching lamps or different lamps of the same height with matching lamp-shades. And, of course, all horizontal spaces should be clutter free. (Don't forget to use your clutter collector.)

In the living room, new matching pillows and an attractive throw can help bring in color and unify the room. If your furniture looks worn, consider buying or making inexpensive slipcovers.

As we've previously discussed, white or neutral paint can give your home a whole light, bright feel. Even if your home doesn't need a new paint job, you might want to lighten various rooms to give them a fresh look. If your home is looking drab, lightening the paint color of the walls and the ceilings will help dramatically. If you want to retain a little color, consider some neutral shade for the walls, such as eggshell, gray, light beige, or a light peach tone, and paint your trim white.

The important thing is that every room has to look special and fresh so the buyer feels good being there.

KEEP PRIVATE INFORMATION
LOCKED AWAY

Our home is our sanctuary, our castle. It's the place where we experience the most intimate moments of our lives. It's also the place where we pay our bills.

Even if you pay every bill on time, I'm quite certain you don't want to share your personal financial information with prospective buyers coming through your house for showings. But beyond that, keeping your papers, credit card bills, medical information, and other personal financial data locked away is even more important now that identity theft has become one of the fastest-growing crimes in America. According to recent reports, someone's identity is stolen about every sixty seconds.

As I was writing this book, I heard from a detective in southern California. He had previously spent twenty-five years with the sex crimes division of the Los Angeles Police Department, and was now working in a community about eighty miles south of the city. I had written a column about how con artists, posing as home buyers, would engage real-estate agents to take them on house showings. While the "husband" or "wife" amused the agent, the other would sweep through the bedrooms and home offices taking whatever was available: jewelry, credit cards, checkbooks, cash, family heirlooms.

It turned out that the detective was then pursuing two sets of home-buyer con artists, and had one of the "wives" in custody.

One couple had hit fifty homes in forty-five days, and had been caught writing checks off a checkbook that had been stolen.

An even bigger danger is probably sitting on a desk in your home office or spare bedroom. When I wrote my first book on selling a home, *100 Questions Every Home Seller Should Ask*, the Internet as we know it today barely existed. Today, most Americans have access to a computer, and a large percentage of homeowners have computers in their homes. High-speed access (via DSL or cable modems) is growing quickly, as more consumers use the Internet to research, shop, and communicate. Many Americans use their home computers to manage their family's finances. Others run small businesses from their homes and use computers to manage the information.

Computers with personal information can put you at risk. People can quickly and easily flip on unlocked computer systems and use it to steal personal financial information. Some people leave lists of passwords taped to their monitors, for when they're searching the Web. Credit card bills left lying out can put you at risk. Checkbooks (particularly if you have your social security number on your checks) can put you in danger.

Although your information should be safe in the privacy of your own home, when you put your home up for sale, you give up a large measure of privacy. You invite strangers to poke through your closets and drawers. Don't give them the opportunity to make your life miserable by stealing from you.

A GOOD START

Are you wondering what can be stolen from a house? It isn't just small stuff. One agent told me she knew of a couple that walked out with a woman's full-length fur coat and never got caught!

If con artists can steal a fur coat in broad daylight, they can certainly conceal a checkbook, cash, jewelry, or your personal financial information.

Start by thinking about where you keep your personal financial records. Where do you keep bills and receipts? Letters and account statements? Spare cash and jewelry? The best place to keep these important items, especially when you're selling your home, is either in a locked safe that is securely bolted to the floor or wall, or in a locked file cabinet at the back of a closet. (Don't keep the key anywhere near the file cabinet.)

You can purchase either a small safe or file cabinet with a lock for a few hundred dollars from any office-supply company. Shop online for the best selection and prices.

If you have a computer with personal financial information on it, you must make sure it is password protected (and don't write your password on a yellow sticky and attach it to the monitor). Better yet, make sure your computer is turned off and perhaps covered with an attractive dustcover. If you have a laptop, unplug it and make sure it is well hidden. Laptops are so light and thin these days that it is easy to simply slip one under a coat and make off with it.

When you have a showing, all jewelry, cash, and family heirlooms should be locked away either in your home safe or stashed somewhere secure. Typically, showings take about twenty minutes. You have to limit any opportunities a thief would have to take items in that time frame.

Clearly, having your personal financial information, or cash, or jewelry, or family heirlooms stolen isn't what you asked for when you decided to sell your home. But thieves and con artists live among us, and if you don't want to be ripped off, you have to take some steps to protect yourself.

Keep in Mind, Other Things Can Be Stolen

When Sam and I were gutting our home, we had a subcontractor who came in to do some work. He seemed spaced out most of the time, and didn't do the work he said he had done. When we finally threw him out, he took one of Sam's expensive professional drill sets.

To some folks, tools and equipment stored in your basement or garage are easy to steal. Others will go after the silver. Prepare your home by thinking ahead about what could be taken during a showing, and then hiding, locking away, or packing away those items.

ORGANIZE YOUR BOOKS, VIDEOS, CDS, AND CD-ROMS

I have several friends who are somewhat compulsive when it comes to organizing items in their house. One friend alphabetizes her spices, books, and CDs. Another friend extended her closet so she could neatly stack DVDs and videos next to her stereo equipment (which would be completely hidden from view).

If you're like me, however, your home isn't perfectly organized twenty-four hours a day. But here's the rub: I know I'd have no trouble organizing someone else's home. Why? Because I'm not psychologically attached to their stuff the way I am to my own.

Whenever I visit my mother's home, I take the opportunity to help her go through some of her things in anticipation of her move next year. By the time she moves, she'll have lived in her home for more than thirty-five years. Anyone would manage to collect a lot of stuff in that period of time, and my mother is no exception. But because it's not my stuff, I don't have any problem at all with giving it away or throwing it away. (My editor, Annik, wanted to know if I consult with my mother before tossing out her stuff. Sometimes, but not always . . .)

Organizing the little things in your home gives the buyer the reassuring feeling that you're in complete control of your space.

A GOOD START

While you don't have to alphabetize everything in your home, it helps to keep things neat and organized.

Start with your bookshelves. If your books are twisted sideways, stacked two rows deep, or overstuffed, take down enough books so that books of similar size can be stacked attractively. Books tend to look best when they are displayed in groups of the same size, with the edges out so that they meet the edge of the bookshelf. That way, all the books appear to be the same size. (For some good examples, look at photos of bookshelves in any decorating magazine, like *Architectural Digest* or *Metropolitan Home.*) If you have an attractive set of coffee-table books (oversize hardcover books with glossy, colorful covers), but you have no available coffee table on which to display them, lay them flat on a shelf so that their spines stick out.

One thing some homeowners don't realize is that you can, and should, leave space on a bookshelf. It's possible, even desirable, to leave some open space—the so-called white space we talked about in previous steps. By using the open space to display one attractively framed photo, or a vase, or a sculpture piece, you're giving the buyer the message that you not only have room to spare, but you know how to make a space attractive, too.

(There is no need for you to disclose to prospective home buyers that you've already packed away ninety-seven boxes of books. This is called Home Seller Magic.)

When it comes to videos, CDs, CD-ROMs, DVDs, and other items that are the same size and shape, you'll want to stack them neatly. Whether you stack them in a bookshelf or purchase a cool-looking CD rack, or stack them on a shelf in a closet somewhere, make sure they look organized. (Alphabetizing is an option, not a requirement, for a successful sale!)

Children's toys have a way of spilling out all over. Although we'll talk about children's spaces later in the book, it's important to keep their toys (whether in the playroom, in their bedroom, or in the family room) confined to one wicker basket or plastic tub. The rest can be packed away or given away if your child has outgrown them.

Kitchens are repositories for all kinds of collections, from spices to salt-and-pepper shakers to olive-oil bottles. Make sure your spices are attractively displayed, if they're out. Better yet, find a drawer and put them all away. If you have to leave out anything, make sure it's an attractive container, or one set of salt-and-pepper shakers. If you need to leave your cooking tools out, find an attractive container for them.

Make sure you take the time to organize all the little items in your bathrooms. Small bottles of perfume, shampoo and conditioner samples from hotels, and a medicine cabinet full of half-empty bottles won't ever look appealing. Take the time to carefully edit these items so that what's left always looks good.

If organizing doesn't come easily to you, and you can't even imagine how to begin, ask your most organized friend to spend an hour with you giving you suggestions on how to do it better in your own home. Like I said, it's always easier to organize when it's someone else's stuff.

TAKE EXTRA PRECAUTIONS IF YOU HAVE SMALL CHILDREN OR INFANTS

Selling your home is tough enough. Selling it while tending to a family with small children or infants will make anyone a little crazy.

Infants and small children pose special challenges for sellers. There is the constant flow of toys that is difficult to keep organized, and there is an equally constant flow of clothes to and from the laundry. Or there may be unpleasant smells emanating from dirty diapers tossed out in your child's bedroom.

When Mark and Amy went to visit an open house, they were amazed at how each of the four children's bedrooms had its own peculiar odor. The infant's room smelled of vomit (the child had been sick the night before); the middle children were in diapers, with that lovely stench permeating the hallways. The older child's door handle was sticky (probably the result of a sloppily eaten lollipop), and his floor looked as though Cheerios had been ground into the carpet. It smelled like leftover lunch.

Of course, it goes without saying that your children (no matter how old they are) shouldn't attend any showings. Children tend to distract buyers, and it doesn't always work to your advantage. I still remember the four-year-old who took my hand at one showing and made a point to steer me around so I could see the "gross, yucky mold" in her dank basement. She was adorable. But I couldn't run fast enough out of her house. If there's no one who can take care of your children during a showing, and you've agreed to be there (if you're selling by owner you'll have to be there), then cancel the showing. That's better than having an unexpected and unwelcome interruption just as you're answering a prospective buyer's question.

No doubt about it, children pose special challenges for home sellers. Your job is to keep them in line while you keep your home clean.

A GOOD START

If you haven't already instituted a "no-eating-outside-the-kitchen" rule for your children, start today. If your child typically drinks a bottle of milk before bed, make sure it comes in a spill-proof container, and then remove the bottle in the morning (or middle of the night) so lost bottles don't start smelling like soured milk. (That's a smell we lived with for weeks until we found a soured milk bottle leaking under the seat in one of our cars—yuck!)

Once you have the children eating in the kitchen, you can steam-clean their rooms. Make sure dirty diapers either go into a diaper disposal unit (which should contain the odor) or are immediately put into a plastic bag and tossed out with the day's garbage. If your child has an accident, clean it all up. Consider hiring a professional carpet and furniture cleaner to thoroughly go over your children's rooms, or hire a steam cleaner unit at a local home-improvement company and do it yourself.

Are your children's toys and clothes thoroughly weeded out? If you have been putting aside too-small clothes or outgrown toys for the "next one" (whether it's yours or the future offspring of a relative or friend), try to get all these clothes out of the way. Either pack them away or give them to your friend or relative to keep children's clutter in check.

If your children are constantly bringing home schoolwork and art projects, take cardboard or plastic boxes and label one for each child. Put each child's work into his or her box. Anything that doesn't fit will have to be tossed out, or perhaps you can allow your child to choose what he or she wants to keep.

Finally, if you have a yard and you have children's toys, you'll undoubtedly end up with children's toys all over the yard. While buyers may be more forgiving when it comes to a messy yard, having toys strewn about the place will make it difficult for you to get out and keep your yard in the kind of shape it should be in to make it shine.

As I've said before, you want to do everything in your power to create an image of an organized, clean, well-functioning household, inside and out, because that's how prospective buyers imagine themselves living in their future home. You're simply meeting their expectations.

So buy a box or an organizer rack for your children's toys. Make sure the kids pick up the yard before they get dessert, a bedtime book, or whatever treat you need to promise in order to keep things clean. By the way, you might try a few "incentives" (bribes) to get your kids to help keep the basement, the attic, the family room or their bedrooms clean. When it comes to selling, whatever makes it easier is probably a good thing—at least temporarily.

IF YOU DON'T WANT TO LEAVE IT, TAKE IT DOWN BEFORE YOU LIST YOUR HOME

A broker in Atlanta once had a client I'll call Patty, who had a beautiful home that she had lived in for about seven years. When she moved there, she brought with her a light fixture that had been installed in the foyer of her previous house. That's where it hung in her new home, as well. When it came time to sell, her agent asked Patty what she wanted to take with her. Patty wrote down that she wanted to take her refrigerator and some book-cases. But she neglected to exclude the fixture in the listing agreement or on the listing sheets handed out to buyers.

Fast-forward to the closing. Patty had moved out the previous day and, of course, had taken the light fixture with her. The buyers discovered this when they went to do their final walk-through. They placed a hurried call to their agent, who called Patty's agent, who called Patty. "But of course I told you that light fixture was coming with me," she said to her agent. The only problem was that it wasn't written down on the listing agreement, or in any listing sheets, or in the contract. Technically, Patty had made off with something that was supposed to go with the house, and the buyers were pretty steamed up about it.

The situation was resolved during the closing. Patty agreed to pay the buyers more than $250, which was the estimated value of the fixture.

The moral of the story? If you're attached to something in your home, and that something is attached to your walls, the ceiling, or the floor of your house, you'd better specify up front, and in writing, that the item is going with you when you sell your home.

But here's a better idea: Why not simply remove the fixture and replace it with something else before you sell your home? That way, the buyer can't be confused about what's being left and what you're taking with you after you sell.

A GOOD START

In most contracts, a fixture is anything that is permanently attached to the home. Common fixtures include built-in bookcases, light fixtures, fireplace mantels, curtains and shades, and built-in pieces of furniture (like a built-in couch or a banquette in the kitchen). In your garden, a swing that is attached to the roof of your enclosed back porch might be considered a fixture, as is a grill that is permanently attached to a gas line.

There are two questions you have to ask yourself when it comes to fixtures:

1. What do I really want to keep?

2. What am I willing to give up to make the sale?

It's all well and good to be married to a particular light fixture. You might want to keep it because you like it, or because the company that produced it has stopped making it. Or you might want to keep a particular light fixture because it's an antique and quite valuable, or because it's a family heirloom. If that's the case, remove it from your home and pack it away before you list your property. Because if a buyer sees it, and falls in love with it, and convinces himself or herself that the house isn't *the house* without it, the deal isn't going to go through until you give up something in return—usually cash.

Walk around your house and mark down all the fixtures you want to keep. When you hire your real-estate agent, make sure he or she knows what is and isn't staying after you move. Put these items down in the listing sheet, and be sure they get written into the contract before you sign it.

Finally, be sure you and your spouse or partner agree on what you're willing to give up to make the right deal happen.

4

Behind Closed Doors: Closets, Cabinets, Pantry, and Storage Spaces

ORGANIZE, ORGANIZE, ORGANIZE

By now, I hope you've tackled cleaning and organizing all the visible surfaces in your home: your kitchen countertop, bookcases, tabletops, nightstands, bathroom countertops, window ledges, and fireplace mantels.

Now it's time to straighten out and organize everything you stuffed behind closed doors.

Why? Home buyers are invariably curious. They think nothing of opening up your medicine cabinet, linen cabinet, and closets, and then get down on their hands and knees to look at what you have stored under your bed. If you think someone won't look under your bed, then you haven't been to enough open houses. (There you can watch home buyers examine the house exactly as they will someday examine yours.)

What should be cleaned out? Anything that can be opened up.

- **In the kitchen:** cabinets (upper and lower), refrigerator, pantry, mop closet.

- **In the bathrooms:** cabinets, medicine chest, linen closet, other closets.

- **In the bedrooms:** closets, built-ins, cabinets, dresser drawers. (Even if you're taking them with you, someone may open them up. So be ready.)

- **In the family room:** cabinets, closets, built-ins, armoires, toy chests.

- **In your home office:** cabinets, closets, built-in file cabinets.

- **In the attic or the basement:** any area that a home buyer would be able to walk into, built-in cabinets, or other storage containers.

- **In the garage:** spaces under the stairs, other built-in storage cabinets with a door on them, shelves and open cabinets, hooks, and so forth.

Besides satisfying a prospective buyer's curiosity (what's really behind that door?) organizing will again create the illusion that there is room to spare in your home for anything your buyer may own.

A GOOD START

When it comes to cleaning out a closet or another space and getting it organized, I subscribe to the following rule: **If you haven't worn it, used it, or thought about it for the past three to five years, pack it away, give it away, or throw it away.**

It's so easy to pack up something, thinking you'll use it again soon. Ten years later, you've completely forgotten about whatever it was, and it's now either moldy, out of date, the wrong size, or completely useless in your life. Or all four.

Be tough on your stuff. When you're cleaning out underneath your bathroom sink, for example, throw away the years' worth of cosmetic mistakes you've made, and the free tubes of hot pink and orange lipstick that you got when you bought an eye shadow a decade ago. Throw away or give away old makeup brushes and the extra electric razor you received for Father's Day seven years ago and only used once. Donate the zillions of tiny bottles of hotel shampoo, soap, conditioner, and sewing kits to a homeless shelter or a battered women's shelter in your area. (You can find them listed in the local phone book, and they will be so grateful.) You might also find other charities that would find these items useful, like your local Salvation Army. If you're not going to use something in the next six weeks, the odds are you won't use it for the next year.

I don't want you to organize yourself right down to a minimalist lifestyle. I don't want you to have to spend thousands of dollars restocking your shelves once you get to your new place. (You'll have to spend thousands of dollars on other things once you get there.) But I do want you to take charge, and not let your stuff control you.

REMOVE HALF THE CLOTHES FROM EACH CLOSET

The 1880s farmhouse Sam and I bought years ago had one small closet in each bedroom upstairs, and two more teeny-tiny closets that had been fashioned out of part of the downstairs hall when someone decided to install indoor plumbing. That was plenty of closet space if all you kept in your closet were a pair of overalls for working in the fields and a "go-to-church" suit for Sundays, funerals, and weddings. Since we each owned more than one suit, it was a pretty tight squeeze for us.

Today, everyone wants more closet space. We need the space to house our clothes, linens, towels, coats, shoes and boots, children's toys and stuffed animals, photographs, boxes of wedding gifts that we haven't used yet, stuff from the previous moves we haven't gotten around to opening, books, and oversize boxes, tubs, and plastic containers of stuff we buy at Sam's Club or Costco, among other items.

Unless your closet goes on forever, you probably have a limited amount of space. The fact that you don't have enough closet space may even be the primary reason you want to sell your home.

If that's the case, you've got a tough challenge ahead. What you need to do is meet your prospective buyer's expectation that you have more than enough closet space for everything they own. Since that can be a tall order, depending on the house, it requires drastic action.

A GOOD START

Open the door to each closet. Look at how much stuff you have hanging from the rod. If it's bending under the weight of all your hanging stuff, that's a bad sign. I've actually had rods break under the weight of hanging clothes.

If you're looking at your clothes closet, start by separating out all the clothes you wear during whatever two seasons have just passed. So, if it's spring, take out your fall and winter garments. If it's winter, take out your summer and fall clothes. Pack away these items, mark the boxes carefully, and store them downstairs in your basement or in a rented storage locker.

Analyze the closet again. Straighten out all the hangers that have gotten caught up with each other, and toss all wire hangers and dry cleaners' plastic bags. Can you hang all the remaining clothes straight and neat? Does your closet now look like a Container Store or California Closets ad? If not, then you'll have to remove another set of clothes or other items.

If you must have the remaining clothes handy, perhaps you need to add storage space to your bedroom. Can you buy an attractive armoire in which to store hanging or folded clothes? Can you replace a chest of drawers with something bigger that will give you more space? I can't emphasize enough how important it is for a buyer to be able to open your closet door and see that you have enough space for what you need to store there. The illusion of having enough (or extra) closet space is a powerful thing.

If you can't add an armoire, consider revamping your closet with inexpensive white wire shelving available from your local home-improvement store. In other words, you'll create a custom-built closet for several hundred dollars.

Call a custom closet installer and have the company send someone out to design and price a closet for you. (Depending on the sales price you hope to get for your home and the size closet you're actually working with, it may be well worth it for you to have the company build the closet for you.) If you like the concept, but the price exceeds your budget, then design your own closet, and buy the raw materials you need at your local home-improvement store. The least-expensive option will likely be white-coated wire shelves that you can have cut to any size you need. (Which is what Sam put into the first condo we owned after we got married.)

In the Pantry

The nice thing about building a closet is that buyers can see exactly where stuff goes. If you have space for a pantry, but it is also disorganized, you may want to use the white wire shelving to give yourself more space, particularly if you're the kind of cook who likes to have plenty of staples and supplies on hand. Use clips attached to the wall to hold your broom and mop. Use a plastic bag holder to keep plastic bags from flying all over the place. Use the soft drink dispenser to maximize the space taken up by cans of soda. Use pull-out shelving for table linens. Pack all the kids' party goods in a plastic tub and store it on the bottom shelf. Install vertical shelving in one area for trays, cookie sheets, cutting boards, and oversize serving pieces.

Under the Sink

If your garbage can normally stays out, look into installing an under-the-sink, pullout wire shelf with a basket inside. While the wastebasket may be smaller than you're used to, requiring you to empty the garbage more frequently, it's better than having a garbage can that sits in the middle of your kitchen, taking up space and contributing its odors.

Unless you have pedestal or wall-mounted sinks, you have another opportunity to make the most of your under-the-sink cabinet space by buying wire baskets or inexpensive plastic tubs in which to keep supplies, extra towels, or children's toys.

Whether a closet is big or small, try to find ways to maximize the space in order to keep the items inside looking organized.

REFOLD TOWELS AND SHEETS IN YOUR LINEN CLOSET

There's something enormously satisfying about having loads of freshly laundered towels sitting next to a clean and inviting bathtub. It invites pleasant thoughts of soaking your troubles away. Stacking a few towels on a stainless-steel towel warmer (plug-in versions are available at stores like Restoration Hardware or online for about a hundred dollars) just adds to the image you've created. Details like that encourage buyers to make offers.

But stacking a few towels in strategic but attractive places in your bathrooms isn't enough. You need to make sure your linen closets and laundry room are organized, as well.

If you're lucky enough to have a linen closet in your upstairs or downstairs hallway, it's a big plus for a home buyer. Having a linen closet makes it easier to keep things together, like sheets and towels, that are used in various places around the house. How you stack and organize that closet will make it seem like an even bigger amenity for the buyer.

If you don't have a linen closet, but you have a laundry room, you may want to install more of the white wire shelving above or on the sides of the laundry room. If you have your washer and dryer in a wide closet, consider installing two or three wire shelves above the appliances in order to maximize the space you need for detergent and cleaning solutions and for additional storage space.

If these spaces already have shelves or cabinets, take a look to see if you've maximized every inch of space. Part of doing that is to keep your towels and linens neatly folded, because organization enhances the illusion of space.

A GOOD START

If you can't keep your linen closet organized, you're probably trying to put too many things in it. Like your other closets, try to remove half the items stored in your linen closet. If that means towels get folded and placed under the bathroom sink or in an attractive basket by the floor of the bathroom, or if you have to purchase a towel shelf to install above the toilet next to the tub, so be it.

It's also helpful to learn how to properly fold a towel. Take a towel and fold it in half. Then fold it in thirds. Then, depending on what size it is, fold it in thirds or in half. Store with the neat, rounded end exposed. Store towels of the same size and shape together.

Even if you remove all your towels, keeping your linen closet organized is tough—unless you send out your sheets to be professionally laundered and steam-pressed. (I actually know people who do this and feel it's worth the twenty-five bucks per week per sheet set.) But if you know how to properly fold sheets, it's a lot easier to keep things organized.

Here's my method: Start with your flat sheet. Fold it in half; then fold it in half again. Fold it into thirds, and then turn the sheet over onto itself to make a nice, neat rectangle. Fitted sheets are a bit more difficult to fold. Start by folding one in half lengthwise, and fit the fitted corners into each other. Next, take the fitted side and fold it a third of the way over. Take the flat side and fold it on top of the fitted side. Then turn the sheet over onto itself to make a neat rectangle that is the same size as the shape you created for the flat sheet. If you like, you can fold the matching pillowcases and store them together with the sheets. Some people actually take the folded sheets, and all but one of the matching pillowcases, and store them inside the final pillowcase (you can turn the pillowcase inside out if you're worried about it getting dirty). That way, when you go to make a bed, your sheets are all together.

For more information on folding linens, check out Martha Stewart's Web site, at MarthaStewart.com.

SIMPLE STEP
21

KEEP YOUR HOME AT A COMFORTABLE TEMPERATURE YEAR-ROUND

On a freezing cold, rainy day, a home buyer is going to want to walk into your home and feel warm. If he or she doesn't immediately feel the warmth emanating from your radiator or furnace, your home won't seem that appealing. The opposite is true on a very hot, humid day. A prospective buyer will want to walk into your home and have it feel crisp and cool.

The temperature at which we keep our homes is an important element for home buyers. While everyone has their own preferences—I have friends who roast at 72°F and others who freeze at the same temperature—it is important for buyers to feel comfortable inside your home. This will help them understand that your home's furnace (or heating or air-conditioning systems) functions correctly.

A GOOD START

Although it may seem wasteful, you'll want to set your thermostat a little higher in winter and a little lower in summer than you might ordinarily do, simply to make sure a prospective buyer is comfortable in your home. For example, you may want to set your thermostat for at least 72°F during winter and at 69°F during summer. Although you'll pay a few dollars more, it's only over a few weeks' or months' time, so the actual cost shouldn't be too great. But the psychological benefit can help your buyer feel much more comfortable with the idea of buying your home.

Vacant Homes

Even if your home is vacant, don't make the mistake of turning off the air-conditioning and heating systems. In the summer, without air-conditioning, a house can quickly grow moldy just from the humidity in the air. A prospective buyer could be treated to the sight of mold growing on your windows, curtains, or walls, which will hardly put him or her in the mood to make an offer. In the winter, homes without heat can quickly turn into messes, with pipes freezing and bursting. You'd quickly have your hands full with repairing your home from the devastation caused by a burst pipe.

The safest course when selling a vacant home is to keep the air-conditioning and heating systems on, but to set them at slightly higher or lower levels, perhaps at 75 degrees for the air conditioner but no lower than 65 degrees during the winter.

5

The Basement, the Attic, and the Garage

DON'T TRY TO HIDE RECURRING PROBLEMS

When George was looking for a home, he went into one house that he liked very much. It appeared that the sellers had taken great pains to make sure everything was freshly painted, cleaned up, and organized. George liked the place so much, he went back a second time. The house still looked fantastic, inside and out.

One of the sellers was pulling into the driveway as George and his agent were coming out the front door to inspect the exterior of the house.

"Have you had any problems with leaking?" George said to the owner. The owner replied that they had had a problem with the basement leaking along the western side of the house, but that it had since been taken care of.

"What was done to fix the problem?" George asked. The owner said that a foundation contractor had come in to reseal the corners and joints.

George went back into the house and decided to look around the basement again. He looked at the west wall, and it seemed clean and dry. He touched the wall, and it felt cold and a little moist. He looked closely at the base of the wall and noticed a little brown stain. A watermark had formed against the white wall.

George went back upstairs and thanked the owner, who was chatting to his agent. "Good news," the agent said. "The seller says the basement has been dry for two years." When George went back to the house for a third visit, a few days later, he imme-diately went to look for the stain in the basement. But it was gone. Another coat of white paint had been applied.

Unsure about whether the house was going to be fine, or expensive to fix, George passed on buying the property. It seemed to him that the sellers were trying to hide something.

Although professional home inspectors can't see behind walls, many have tools like double-pronged moisture readers that can tell them whether there is moisture in a wall or ceiling, and small socket plug-ins that reveal if the wiring has been done correctly. They have equipment they carry that helps them test the draw of your hot-water heater vent and if there is any gas escaping from your furnace. Years of experience help the best home inspectors place educated guesses about what's really going on behind the fresh coat of paint, the carpet they can't pull up, or the heavy fur-niture placed strategically against the foundation wall.

Few states license professional home inspectors, but the orga-nization that does some of the most thorough training is the American Society of Home Inspectors (ASHI), located in Arlington Heights, Illinois. ASHI requires its members to take classes, to pass a tough exam, and to go on 250 inspections before certification. But just because a professional home inspector is a member of ASHI doesn't necessarily mean he or she is a top inspector. ASHI is a nonprofit trade organization that doesn't police wayward members. To find a top inspector, you have to look for someone who is bonded and insured, who has years of experience, and who comes with a few good recommendations. A good inspector will help you to identify and address recurring problems before you list your home. Log onto ashi.org for a referral to a home inspector near you.

It isn't worth hiding things from home buyers. If the inspector catches something, the buyer is likely to try to renegotiate the purchase price. If the buyer discovers something after closing, and can prove you knew about the problem or should have known, you may be on the receiving end of a lawsuit.

A GOOD START

If you have an ongoing problem with your home, investigate ways in which to have it resolved. If you have a persistent leak, but only during heavy rainstorms, you may need to caulk around the outside of your home. If your roof leaks, you may need to have a roofer come and replace shingles or flashing. If you have water dripping from a ceiling under a bathroom, you may need to regrout the shower or bathtub.

If you catch these problems quickly, before they turn into long-term structural issues, they're usually easy to fix. Trying to hide problems, big or small, is difficult enough, and almost impossible to get away with. Don't even try. (Even the threat of building litigation can be enough to chase away a prospective buyer. One condo owner found himself without an offer after he failed to disclose to the buyer that the building was chasing the developer over a few different issues. The buyer rescinded the offer.)

Keep Your Paperwork

If you have to buy something to fix a problem, or hire someone to do it, be sure to keep the receipt in your house file as proof that the work was actually completed. If there is a problem down the line, your paper trail can help you prove that you thought the issue was resolved.

One way to keep your paperwork organized is to purchase a small plastic file cabinet ($35 or less at your local office-supply store or online), or plastic tub (even cheaper, at five to nine bucks each) with about $10 worth of hanging files (they come in designer colors these days) and manila folders. Use a separate folder to get your receipts, bills, warranties, appliance paperwork, and other house-related documents in order. Each house, condo, or town house you live in should have its own separate filing system. When you close and move into a new house, pack up the files in a plastic tub, and start fresh with your new home.

(See Step 23 for information on seller disclosure, and what the law requires you to tell a prospective buyer about the true condition of your home.)

DISCLOSE HIDDEN ISSUES AND PROBLEMS UP FRONT

Twenty years ago, a major theme of real estate was caveat emptor, which is Latin for "let the buyer beware." In other words, the onus was placed upon the buyer to seek out as much information as possible about the house and the seller before making an offer. Of course, the agent wasn't a big help, since at that time all agents technically worked for the seller. If an agent took a home buyer to see ten properties in a single day, the agent literally worked for ten sellers. The buyer had no representation, no one to help him or her figure all this stuff out.

My, how things have changed. Today, most sellers are required to disclose any problems with their homes (also called "defects") that they know about, or should have known about. These problems must be "material," which means they could affect the value of the home or cost a substantial amount to fix. And you must disclose problems that you know about that can't be seen with the naked eye.

Here are some examples of material defects that should have been disclosed, but weren't.

When Beth and Tom bought their eighty-year-old Victorian home, the sellers failed to disclose that there was asbestos in the basement. They successfully sued the sellers for failing to disclose the asbestos problem, and recovered attorney's fees as well as the cost of the removal and disposal of this hazardous substance.

When Ellyn and Susanna bought their house, the fan from one of the bathrooms vented in the attic instead of outside. That meant the moisture from the bathroom got trapped in the attic, instead of venting outside. The seller claimed that the bathroom vented outside, although he knew differently. Ellyn and Susanna found mold in the attic, a problem that was augmented by a leak in the roof.

The Smiths spent a lot of time scraping down and painting their hundred-year-old home. What they didn't do was fix the crack in the foundation. When they tried to sell their home, two separate buyers got far enough along to hire a professional home inspector. The foundation failed both inspections, and both buyers backed out of the deal. Instead of disclosing the problem, the Smiths carried on as if nothing were wrong. They finally sold their house for a lot less than they wanted, and it was eventually torn down.

Brian's seller told him that the house had central air. Unfortunately, after Brian moved into the house, he discovered that the air-conditioning went into only one room. The inspector missed the problem, and Brian got stuck with the bill.

In most states, the law requires you to disclose any known defects in writing to the buyer. To make it easier, many states have a seller-disclosure form you fill out and sign. The form contains questions about your property, to which you have to answer either yes, no, or don't know. Each state's form is a little different, and some forms are longer than others. In California, for example, you'll have to fill out a six-page Transfer Disclosure Statement. In Illinois, the form is one page with a few dozen questions.

If you lie about something that's wrong with your house, you could be committing fraud, which is serious. In some states, the buyer can recover his or her attorney's fees, in addition to damages in litigation against the seller. That's why the best policy is to simply come clean about any problems that you have with your home.

A GOOD START

Sellers are typically required by law to provide a written disclosure to buyers. In some states, this happens after an agreement has been reached over the price, but in others it is given to the buyers when they are shown the house. Since you're going to need to hand it over, you might as well fill out the form ahead of time.

Ask your agent to give you a copy of the seller-disclosure form that is used in your state. Read the questions carefully. You are not generally required to disclose anything that is public information. For example, if the state has held hearings and decided to put a major interstate one block behind your house, and the buyer isn't aware of it, you may not need to disclose this information. You also may not need to disclose that a subdivision, a strip mall, or an apartment building will be going up, or that next year your property taxes are supposed to double. These items are a matter of public record, and it's the buyer's responsibility to be aware of them. However, if your home has an oil tank, and you know it's there, but it's buried below the tulip bed, you'll need to disclose that.

Disclosure as a Negotiation Tool

If you make a full disclosure to the buyer, he or she should not then be able to come back and ask to renegotiate the agreement based on something the home inspector found. By being up front, you may be able to avoid some or all of those negotiations. (Whether you choose to do something will depend on the strength of the market and whether you're willing to lose this buyer.)

If you don't know about the condition of your home—if, for example, you inherited the property or had it rented out as an investment—you may want to hire a professional home inspector to do a prelisting inspection before you hire a real-estate agent. See Step 33 for details on a prelisting inspection.

SIMPLE STEP
24

CLEAN OUT YOUR GARAGE

Many new homes are offered with attached three- and four-car garages. It's difficult to imagine average Americans owning that many cars.

In fact, many don't. What they do have is a lot of other stuff—like carriages, boats, strollers, lawn mowers, snowblowers, lawn tractors, bicycles, kids' toys, gardening equipment, chairs, sleds, sporting equipment, umbrellas, and, in the off season, outdoor furniture. And all that stuff needs to be stored somewhere.

But Americans are also buying bigger cars, like minivans, SUVs, station wagons, pickup trucks, and the mother of all vehicles, the Chevrolet Suburban. Between bigger cars and more stuff, home buyers are looking for as big a garage as possible. If you have only a two-car garage (like most of us), you'll want to clean out your garage and find a way to max out as much storage space as possible.

Having a big, clean garage will be a real plus for any home buyer.

A GOOD START

The first (and only!) time Sam and I tried to hold a garage sale, almost no one showed up. True, it was the weekend after the terrorist attacks on September 11, 2001, but we had already advertised in the local paper, sorted out our stuff, and arranged it for the sale. And so, hoping for the best, we decided to go ahead with it. After factoring in our advertising costs, we cleared about $100. The best part was sitting out in the sunshine for most of a Saturday morning. The worst part was dragging out all our stuff and then having to haul it back in after we hardly sold any of it.

But I do know people who have held very successful garage sales. Every time my friend Lori hosts a garage sale, she pockets $500 at least. In fact, they can be a great way to turn your junk into profit. It happens all the time.

If you're inclined to hold a garage (or tag) sale, try doing it yourself. There are professional companies that will handle bigger and better sales, like estate sales, although that can be expensive. If you're interested in finding a professional company to handle your sale, look in the paper under the garage-sale and tag-sale ads, and check out the big ads placed by local companies that handle this sort of business. Visit several of these sales and take note of what the people running the sale are doing, and how they're doing it. Ask for their card, and then interview the company about what work they will and will not do, how they price items, how much they take as their cut, and the general hours involved in a sale. Then ask them to come to your home and take a look at what you have. If you have valuable items you're selling, like a grand piano and furniture sets, a company may agree to handle your sale.

But if you don't have enough stuff to interest a professional sales company, consider asking your neighbors to join you so you can run ads for a multifamily garage sale. Buzzwords include "kids' toys and clothing" and "piano." Make sure your ad runs in your local newspaper at least a day or two before you want to hold the sale.

Price your stuff to sell. At the end of the day, if it's still lying around, you're going to have to get rid of it somehow. You can always call a local charity like the Salvation Army and schedule a pickup for the afternoon of your garage sale, or the next week, once you've had a chance to see what's left.

Once you've either sold or given away the stuff you don't want, it's time to get your garage organized. You can purchase inexpensive metal shelving at your local home-improvement center. Try to get things off the floor of the garage. Purchase something that will hold your gardening utensils, even if it's just a large plastic container. You can get inexpensive garden-tool stands from stores like Wal-Mart, Target, or Frank's or something more stylish (and expensive) from stores like Gardener's Eden, Restoration Hardware, Williams-Sonoma, or any number of catalog or online gardening stores. If your garage has a high ceiling, consider buying pulleys to get your bicycles off the floor, or purchase the hardware to keep your bicycles attached to the walls of your garage.

Do you keep your garbage inside your garage? We used to do that because if we left it outside, even if we put several bungee cords across the top, raccoons and other animals would topple over the cans, get inside the garbage, and make a huge mess. A few years ago, we bought several large Rubbermaid storage bins. One is big enough to hold two garbage cans inside it. The top and front open, so if you wanted to, you could keep your garbage outside (where it won't smell up the garage and house) and easily put the cans on the curb for garbage pickup. We bought a smaller matching Rubbermaid storage bin to store our recyclables, and a super-size one for our wheelbarrow, extra garden hoses, and equipment for our lawn tractor.

Once your garage is organized, use a leaf blower to really get all the dirt, dust, and leaves out. If you don't have a leaf blower, and can't borrow one from a friend or neighbor, then sweep the floor clean. (Don't forget to sweep out the cobwebs at the top corners of the garage, too.) Some sellers seal their garage floor against stains. I'm not sure this adds as much value to your home as getting your garage as clean and as organized as possible, but it will make your garage floor look great.

MAKE YOUR ATTIC OR CRAWL SPACE ACCESSIBLE

On a visit one day to a slightly derelict house that was for sale, I attempted to crawl up into the attic. After taking a few steps up a rickety ladder, I gave up, content to peek inside with a flashlight. From what I could see, the attic was dusty and too stuffed with the owner's garbage to make clear what was really there.

Some homeowners like to clean out their attics; others don't. When our friends Leo and Genna were selling their first home, Genna would absolutely not climb into the attic (which was really a crawl space) to toss out old luggage and other things that had accumulated up there over the nearly ten years they had lived in the house. So my husband, Sam, went up there and cleaned out the attic. Genna was thrilled, especially when one of the prospective buyers asked to see what was up there.

In our own house, a farmhouse built in the 1880s, we were able to determine almost the exact age of the house when our professional home inspector, who was also an architect with an interest in historic buildings, was able to crawl into the then unheated space below our first-floor sunroom. He could see the natural face of the unpainted brick used to sheathe the first floor of the house. "It's yellow," he yelled to us from around the corner. "It's what was commonly used to build these homes in the early 1880s."

Getting into tight spaces is a talent every home inspector should have. Giving them access to spaces like attics and crawl spaces, however, is the seller's job.

And access is important. While it's true that your home may have problems which access to these spaces would uncover, you're trying to sell your home, and house hunters have a right to know what they're buying. By making access easier, you not only give buyers the ability to look, but you also dispel their ever-present concern that you're trying to hide something. And, of course, being honest about the true condition of your home is the best policy you can follow when selling.

But some sellers do hide things. One home seller in a suburb far west of Chicago was able to hide the fact that for years, his sewage spewed out into the garden. (Yes, the neighbors always wondered why his grass and garden were so exceptionally green and gorgeous, not to mention smelly at certain times during the year.) To mask the smell inside, the seller left every window wide open during the dead of winter, with the heat blasting. (That should have raised a few red flags for any home buyer.) Later, the buyers discovered that the crawl space was actually filled with a foot of raw sewage. They eventually abandoned the property and went into bankruptcy.

A GOOD START

Make sure every part of your home is accessible to home buyers and their agents. If the original pulldown ladder to the attic doesn't work properly or is unsafe, install a new ladder or fix the old one. Just make sure it's installed safely, as you may be held responsible for any accident that occurs while you own the property.

Your basement crawl space should also be accessible. If you regularly keep the door locked to prevent small children from finding their way down there, give the agent the key, or add a latch higher up on the door (out of the reach of kids) that can be opened by an adult. And if you keep mousetraps in your crawl space or basement, be sure to check them before each showing. There's nothing less appealing than a dead mouse in a house, unless it's a live mouse stuck to a trap. (Better yet, consider removing the traps during the showings. You can put them out again after the buyers leave.)

Finally, it's not enough to have these spaces simply be accessible. The prospective buyer also needs to see what's inside. If you don't have electricity in these spaces, hang a flashlight or two just inside the door or at the top of the stairs so buyers will have the means to see what's inside.

Often, attics and crawl spaces allow a good behind-the-walls look at a home. How the underside of your roof looks can help an inspector figure out not only if your roof was installed correctly, but also if there has ever been any damage and what might have caused it. Some crawl spaces are used to house the mechanical systems for a house (including the water heater, the boiler, the air-conditioning, and the heating), and can reveal quite a bit about how regular the maintenance has been for the entire house.

So keep access to these spaces open and easy for buyers, agents, and inspectors. Again, easy access helps dispel any mystery that can surround these parts of a home.

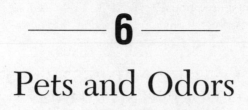

6

Pets and Odors

KEEP YOUR PET RESTRAINED
DURING SHOWINGS

It's hard to imagine someone not liking Brando, a massive German shepherd dog with a heart of gold. Unfortunately, Brando looked like he could take your head off in a single gulp. So his owners, Marya and Tim, kept him in a large cage any time guests came over.

At least he was kept caged. When Phyllis and Ian went to see a prospective home for sale, they could hear ferocious barking from behind the front door. The agent, who had unlocked the door, sat down on the front steps.

"I'm not going in," she said. "But I'm told he's a pussycat once he gets to know you."

If you want to sell your home and you have a pet, be prepared to keep your pet in a cage whenever anyone may be touring your home. There are several reasons why you should keep your pet caged, all of which may be difficult for animal lovers to understand:

1. Many people don't like animals.

2. Some people are afraid of, or phobic about, large animals, especially dogs but often cats, as well.

3. Many people are allergic to animals.

4. Many buyers harbor suspicions that pets do lasting damage to property, and they may assume that the damage is expensive and time-consuming to correct.

5. It's a real turnoff to have an unsuspecting home buyer tour your home only to step in a little "gift" that the pet has left in a strategic spot like the basement floor.

Here's the rest of Phyllis and Ian's story. They finally got into the house with the huge, barking dog because Phyllis was brave enough to walk in (enormously foolish—I'd have hightailed it out of there) and see if she could let the dog out into the backyard. Surprisingly, this worked, and they went in to tour the house. When Phyllis and Ian went into the basement, the lights weren't working. All the carpet had been pulled up because, the agent said, the owners had had a little trouble with water and were replacing the carpet. So Phyllis stepped off the bottom step in her good shoes and went *squish*. She slid across the floor. What had happened was this: The German shepherd had been allowed to roam freely all over the house, but was clearly not housebroken. It had left droppings all over the basement floor. Once her eyes adjusted to the dark, Phyllis could see the little blobs waiting for her all over the basement. As it turned out, the blobs were elsewhere in the house, as well. Needless to say, she and Ian didn't make an offer.

You're never going to win over a non–pet lover. But by keeping your pet caged during showings, you'll allow prospective buyers to have easy access without challenging deeply held fears or beliefs. You'll allow them to relax in your home, enough perhaps to make an offer.

A GOOD START

When selling your home, it's a good idea to create a separate space that looks like the "pet" space in your home. Keeping a cage with a mat and some toys in the kitchen near the water and food bowls will create the illusion that your pet stays in one place rather than roaming freely all over the house. (Undoubtedly, this isn't true, and you should own up to that fact if asked directly.)

If you can't control your pet, or if you have an animal that is too large to be caged up for hours at a time, consider boarding your pet during the day for the few months in which you're showing and selling your home. If you don't have friends or family willing to take your animal, and if a professionally run kennel is beyond your budget, consider hiring a dog walker who can take your pet out for walks before a showing starts and bring him back after the showing ends.

IF YOU HAVE A PET, OR IF YOU SMOKE, CLEAN YOUR HOME AGAIN

All the pet owners I know insist that their pets don't smell. Of course, that's not true. All animals smell, though what they smell of may change depending on the day and date of the last shampooing. Some animals (and as I write this I'm smiling, thinking of my in-laws' former family dog named Tritoe) have such bad breath you'd do anything to avoid being near them.

In the beginning, you might be able to smell your dog or cat. But after a while, your senses become used to the smell, and you may lose some, or all, of your ability to distinguish the smell of your animal.

Smokers also can lose their ability to distinguish certain smells. Often, a smoker who used to smoke inside the house but now only smokes outside still cannot tell whether the inside of the home smells of smoke. The truth is that the walls, the couches, the chairs, and the rugs all retain the scent of smoke, which permeates everything.

Does your home smell of dog? Or cat? Or any other animal you happen to have? Or does it smell of smoke? Even the Saturday-night cigar can leave a long-term residue.

When it comes to animals, it's safe to say that most fish don't smell, although the tank, if left uncleaned, might smell a bit rancid after a while. (The same is true for turtles.) But dogs and cats do smell, and their food bowls, beds, and cages smell, too. And if your cat has a litter box, you'll have to work doubly hard to keep that from smelling.

Of course, what you're working so hard to do is to keep your animal's natural smell from clouding the judgment of a prospective buyer, who perhaps is not an animal lover or is, like my husband, allergic. Many individuals are antismoking fanatics who will immediately cross your house off their list if they detect even a whiff of smoke.

Other odors can be a huge turnoff for buyers, including the noxious "poopy-diaper" smell, vomit, and even alcohol.

A GOOD START

Does your home smell? You probably can't tell any longer, so invite a few objective people (who don't own animals, smoke, or have infants at home) to walk into your house and tell you how it smells, what it smells of, and where the smells are coming from.

Before you can begin cleaning, you have to rid your home of the source of the smell. (And no, I'm *not* suggesting you throw out your animals or infants!)

When it comes to animals, wash or change the cloth case on their sleeping beds. Thoroughly clean out their cages, and run their food and water bowls through the dishwasher. If the cat litter smells, either change it more frequently or try a different brand. (There are even machines that will self-scoop litter and keep it in an enclosed space until it can be emptied.)

If your animals have peed on the carpet and wood floors for a long time, your home may be very difficult to clean. You may not only have to replace the carpet, but also sand down the wood floors to get rid of the smell. In one situation, a home buyer had to replace the floorboards because the former owner's cats (five or six of them) had destroyed it over a number of years, and there was no other way to rid the house of the stench. Painting the walls and steam-cleaning your furniture will help, too.

If you smoke indoors, stop doing so immediately. If you've smoked for a long time, your walls and furniture may have picked up the smell. Like the procedure for animal smells, smoke smells may require you to clean or replace the carpet and repaint the interior of your home. Smoke often permeates the fabric on your chairs and sofas. Consider steam-cleaning these to get rid of smoke smells.

Once you've recleaned your home, invite your objective friends or neighbors in to give your home a final sniff. If they still smell something, try to identify where the smell is coming from. Then try to work out why the smell is still there and what can be done about it.

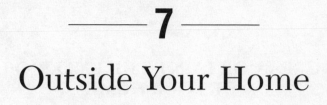

7

Outside Your Home

CLEAN OR PAINT THE EXTERIOR
OF YOUR HOME

Technology has changed the way people buy homes. Today, you can log on to the Internet at any time and view approximately 1 to 1.5 million listings. You can view homes that are listed in your local multiple listing service (MLS), or those that are for sale by owner. Most sellers end up listing their homes on the Internet, either through their agent's personal, company, or franchise Web site.

Almost all these Web pages feature digital photographs of the home listed. Some of the photographs will be 360 degrees, which allows the buyer to feel as though he or she were standing in the middle of a room, turning around to see everything in it. Other sites feature short video tours of the interior and exterior of the home. (For a longer discussion of technology that sellers should know about and consider using, see Step 35.)

Research shows that at least 75 percent of home buyers now start their search for a home on the Internet at sites like Realtor.com and HomeAdvisor.com, where they can easily click on the photos of different homes that meet their space, amenity, or price criteria. First impressions are powerful, and the first opportunity you may have to impress a home buyer is a digital photo of the exterior of your home on the Web. So it's crucial to pay attention to how the exterior looks.

Once buyers decide your home is worth seeing, their agent will often give them the address. Buyers will then do what I call a drive-by showing. That is, they slowly drive by your home, trying to decide if they like it enough to spend the time to see the inside. You have approximately six to ten seconds (the approximate time it takes a car to pass from lot line to lot line) to impress the buyer enough to stop and take another look. If that second look (the first was probably the Internet photo) impresses a buyer, the agent will call to set up an appointment to see the interior of your home.

The bottom line is that you've got to make your home's exterior shine. If it doesn't, you could lose a potential offer and not even know it.

The first thing to do is to clean or paint the exterior of your home. Why? Homes that are well cared for are particularly attractive to home buyers.

Doing the proper maintenance on a home is both expensive and time consuming. If you've done the work, a prospective home buyer knows there won't be much to do for at least the first few years, saving time *and* money. Agents say that buyers, often pressed for time and cash, are sometimes willing to pay more for a home that's in perfect or near-perfect condition because it saves them so much time and aggravation down the line.

A GOOD START

Different types of exterior cladding require different maintenance regimes.

- **Brick.** Brick homes need to be tuck-pointed about once every fifteen years to prevent water infiltration through cracks in the mortar. If your home hasn't been tuck-pointed in that time, and is in such bad shape you can see the chinks in the mortar, consider tuck pointing before you list your home. If your brick face has been painted, you'll need to paint or whitewash it every few years. If you're allowing someone else's paint to wear off your bricks, you may want to look into applying a chemical peel, which will hasten the removal of the paint.

- **Clapboard.** If your home is made of wood clapboard, and is painted or stained, and you haven't repainted it in a number of years, you should seriously consider doing so before you list it. Before you start, check the house to be sure all the wood is in good condition. Replace any rotting boards or lintels. If you're thinking about changing the color of the house, remember this: Many people prefer homes that are painted white or earth tones. You should also paint any outbuildings (garages, barns, toolshed) so that the colors match or blend with the house colors. To find good house colors, walk or drive through your neighborhood to see which homes appeal to you. One thing to keep in mind: Stains generally last longer than paint. Less future maintenance could be a strong sales pitch for home buyers.

- **Shingles.** If you have a house with shingles, and you've stained them, great. They'll probably look wonderful. However, inspect your house to make sure none of the shingles have blown away or rotted out. Make sure each shingle looks as good as the others. If one is damaged or missing, be sure to replace it before you stain or paint.

- **Vinyl or aluminum siding.** If you want to have a home that's less work, consider cladding your next home in vinyl or aluminum. If you're selling a home that's clad in vinyl or aluminum siding, you may want to have the exterior of your house or town home power-washed to bring out the color of the siding and give it a crisp, clean look. Before you start power washing, inspect your siding for any cracks or gaps. You may need to reseal certain areas, especially around the windows, or any place where moisture has worked its way inside the house.

- **Hard coat stucco.** Real stucco, also known as hard coat stucco, is a cementlike exterior that is hand-applied like plaster over a metal lathe. Hard coat stucco can crack, but it is generally thought to be extremely durable. If your stucco looks dirty, you may want to paint it. If it has chipped or cracked, you can hire a hard coat stucco contractor to come out and repair it before you repaint.

- **Synthetic stucco.** If your home is clad with synthetic stucco, you should to hire an inspector who specializes in synthetic stucco to do a full exterior inspection every six months to a year to make sure the cladding stays in good condition. If the exterior cladding is in good condition, there's little you'll want to do to the exterior, other than try to clean it up a bit. If you need repair work done, it's best to do it before you put your house on the market.

WASH YOUR WINDOWS

If you want to bring a little sunshine into your home, try washing your windows—both the regular ones and your storm windows.

Dirty windows can greatly reduce the amount of light that filters into your home. And when you look outside, the dirt, grime, and water stains that accumulate on windows over time can make it difficult to see the view. Dirty windows also send a message about your cleanliness (or the lack thereof) to the buyer.

From the outside, dirty windows don't seem to sparkle as much as they could. If you have filthy storms and screens, crawling with bugs and covered with spider webs, it's not going to impress a prospective buyer or his or her agent—who may have other buyers interested in seeing your home.

A GOOD START

If you have newer windows that click out for easy cleaning on the outside, you may be able to wash them yourself. If your windows don't open, or if they don't open easily, you may want to hire a window-washing company to do the job properly.

If you have storms and screens up in your windows, have the window washers take them down ahead of time. (You can leave them up and pay the window washers to take them down and put them back, but it may be expensive.) You can clean the screens by brushing them down or washing them with a hose. If you have a leaf blower, you can try blowing dust and grime off the screens. It's easiest to clean storm windows while they are on the ground. Have your window washers put them back into place after your windows are washed.

Make sure the window-washing company you hire is licensed (if appropriate in your state), bonded, and insured. Check out the company for complaints on the Better Business Bureau's site (www.bbb.org). You may also want to ask the company for references. Remember, don't pay for the job up front. Have the company do the windows, and then pay the bill, or come up with a plan to pay just 10 or 20 percent down at the beginning, with the rest paid when the job is completed.

SIMPLE STEP
30

MAKE OVER YOUR LANDSCAPING

When you walk down the street, what do you notice about a property? If you're like most people, your eyes will be drawn to a beautiful front garden, brightly colored window boxes, and planted pots. Thick, weed-free green grass is also a winner, especially if the owner has taken the trouble to cut the grass in an interesting path.

You can clean up, repaint, re-tuck-point, and redo your exterior all you like. But when you're selling your home, an unkempt garden may be the thing to discourage a buyer from falling in love with—and making an offer for—your home. On the other hand, a gorgeous garden, one that takes full advantage of the various seasons, will be perceived as inviting. Indeed, buyers are more likely to stop by a colorful garden that is weeded and neat, if for nothing else than to get some good ideas for their own gardens.

Make time and set aside enough money to make over your landscape. If you're a good gardener and have taken excellent care of your landscaping, you can probably do this yourself. If not, you may want to hire a professional to come in and give your yard an upgrade, including trimming hedges, mowing the lawn, edging your flower beds, and trimming your trees.

All this trimming may even help increase the light in your house. Often, landscaping overgrows to such a degree that it blocks the light from coming into your home. When making over your garden, be sure to remove any landscaping obstructions, including trimming back errant tree branches and hedges, cutting back plants in window boxes, and removing overgrown ivy. If you have huge trees growing right up against the house, consider hiring a landscape company to remove them and replant the yard with more house-friendly trees, whose roots will not damage your foundation or sewer lines.

Flaunt whatever your garden offers. For example, if you have southern exposure, plant colorful flowers that will take full advantage of the sun's rays. If you have a shade garden, plant different varieties of hostas that will attract the eye. Attractive containers can add form and color in the right area. You might also try hanging a few colorful baskets in the summer or putting up a decorative wreath in fall or winter months.

A GOOD START

If you're selling during spring and summer, it may pay to have a local landscape company (or gardening center) come in and do a design for a season or two of nonstop color. Then, no matter when a home buyer stops by, your garden will be ready.

If you've had leaking in your basement, now would also be a good time to regrade your landscaping away from the house, to help drain water away from the basement walls. You can then reseed the grass or, if you're selling soon, put in a little sod over the affected areas. (Just don't forget to water it!)

Driveways and Walkways

Your property's landscape also includes your driveway. If yours is asphalt, consider having it seal-coated so that it has that dark, well-maintained look. If your driveway or sidewalk is cracked, price out the cost of fixing the concrete. If it's beyond repair, you may want to redo the entire walkway or driveway. But check first with your agent to see if doing either of these projects will raise your estimated sales price or enable you to get the price you want faster.

If you live in a condominium, co-op, or town house, the landscaping surrounding your unit may not be your responsibility. But if you do have outdoor space, make the most of it. If your condo or co-op has a balcony, make sure you either have attractive window boxes or pots filled with a colorful arrangement of flowers or natural grasses. If the area is big enough to sit in, offer an attractive table and chairs. If your town house has a small patio, make sure your landscaping is artfully arranged and makes the space seem colorful, peaceful, and inviting. If you live in a maintenance-free development, make sure you don't need permission from the association board to add a few colorful flowers around the entrance to your unit. If you live in a multistory building, you may want to put a colorful plant outside your front door. (You could use a lifelike silk arrangement.) Another option might be an attractive umbrella stand.

Lights

Your house should be well lit at night, for beauty as well as safety. Make sure your safety lights over the driveway have bulbs. You can put your front and back lights on a timer. (If you're going to be away for an extended period of time while your house is on the market, you should install a few timers in various places in the house so it appears that you're home at different times.)

It's also important to have a light shining on or near your home's street number. Potential buyers will drive by at twilight or even in the dark, to see what your house looks like inside from the outside. Having your street number illuminated will make it much easier to find.

Planning Ahead

If you're going to sell your home several seasons from now, you have an opportunity to plan ahead to give your garden a little extra "curb appeal." In the fall, plant extra bulbs to provide a pop of color early in spring. In spring, plant late-fall blooming bulbs and bushes or shrubs that will turn a beautiful shade of orange or red. Choose flowers that will give you maximum impact for the minimum amount of money.

Winter

If you live in a cold-weather climate, snow, ice and freezing rain is to be expected. Buyers may want to get into your home to take a look, but if the walk and the driveway haven't been cleared, they aren't going to be able to get there easily.

Make sure your walkway and driveway are plowed as soon as possible after a snowfall. Liberally sprinkle salt whenever the weather gets near freezing. (You don't want to be sued by someone who slipped and fell on your driveway.) If salt is banned in your area because of drinking water runoff, use sand, birdseed, or other materials recommended by your local home-improvement store.

If ice dams (huge frozen icicles that hang over the edge of your gutters, which are caused by large amounts of snow that freeze and melt repeatedly) tend to form on your house, use the summer and fall months preceding the sale to install a heat coil that will keep your roof ice free all winter long. You want your home to stand out because it's in excellent shape, not because it has the biggest roof icicle in the neighborhood.

Gutters

While it's difficult for a home buyer to peer into gutters to see if they're clean, sometimes birds build nests that are visible from the street. Keeping your gutters clean makes good sense, as well. If it rains while a home buyer is touring your home, and your gutter starts overflowing, the one thing the buyer may remember about your house is that you have a problem with the gutters. That could effectively eliminate your house from contention.

DISPLAY A "FOR SALE" SIGN

Sam and I once bought a condo as an investment. About nine months later, our tenant moved out, and we tried to rent the condo. When we bought the unit, "for sale" and "for rent" signs were permitted. Nine months later, the condo association had voted to outlaw all signs. I'm convinced that not being able to put out a "for rent" sign made it much more difficult to rent the condo. While we had the condo listed with a local agent, having a sign in the ground would have helped tremendously.

Eventually, we rented our condo, but I'm convinced that we lost a few extra months of rent simply because the condo association didn't permit us to put a "for rent" sign in the front yard.

Placing a large "for sale" sign in your front yard is a crucial bit of advertising you should take advantage of when you sell your home. If you're selling by owner (also known by the acronym FSBO, which is pronounced "fizz-bo" and stands for "for sale by owner"), it's even more important, since you probably don't have your property listed in the local MLS.

If "for sale" signs are not permitted in your condo or town-house development, you may have to talk to your homeowner's association to see why the signs were banned and what can be done about temporarily lifting the ban (which may or may not be possible). In the case of our investment condominium, too many units were either for sale or for rent at the same time, and members of the board were nervous that having the signs out in front would stigmatize the building. (Actually, eliminating signs is one of the things that cause brokers and agents to start bad-mouthing a property, because it makes their job harder.)

Some neighborhoods, towns, villages, and homeowner's associations ban "for sale" signs even in front of single-family homes. Check out the local law at your village, city, or town hall. If your town or subdivision has rules against displaying a "for sale" sign for a house, a car, or a boat, you could be risking a huge fine, not to mention angering the local law enforcement. While signage is important, it's not worth being fined.

A GOOD START

Your sign should have several important pieces of information: It should say the house is "for sale" in large, easy-to-read type. It should contain a phone number, also in large type so people passing in their cars can quickly write it down or dial it on their cell phones. If you have a Web site for your property, you should list that, as well. And if the house is going to be open over the weekend, you should be able to hang an "Open Sunday 1 to 4" (or whatever time your open house will be) sign off the top or bottom of the sign.

Where do you get a sign? You have three choices.

- **Hire a broker.** You can hire a full-service or discount brokerage firm, which will then place a sign in your front yard. If you live in an apartment building, the agent may put a sign out in front of the building or not. It's different for each condo complex.

- **Make a sign.** You can make a sign, either by nailing a couple of pieces of wood together and painting them, or going to a local sign store (Kinko's makes signs on plastic), and then attaching it to a piece of wood.

- **Buy a sign.** You can buy a "for sale" sign from a local stationery or hardware store, a sign shop, a large retailer like Kmart or Wal-Mart, or even online. Many FSBO sites offer signage for sale. (See Step 37 for a few suggestions on FSBO and discount brokerage Web sites you may want to check out. And since Web sites go in and out of business so frequently, be sure to start your search at Google.com.)

If you're selling by owner, the best deal will probably be to hire a discount brokerage firm, which for $500 or less will list your property in the local MLS, and provide you with all the signage you need, including "open house" signs. While you can purchase a fairly inexpensive sign, you might get more for your money this way. Once again, the most important piece of information is your telephone number. Make sure anyone can read the number easily from the street.

LIMIT YOUR HOLIDAY AND FAMILY DECORATIONS

When my son, Michael, turned three, he fell in love with Christmas lights. But he couldn't understand why all our neighbors took their lights down and put them away in January. Because there are a couple of houses near where we live that keep holiday lights and decorations up all year, he made a point of letting me know we were passing the "house with the lights" every time we drove by.

Holidays lights, signs, posters, balloons, and streamers are all fun to put up—and perhaps not so much fun to take down. And there are holidays to celebrate almost every month of the year.

But when you're selling your home, less is definitely more. Holiday decorations, if overdone, can get in the way of a buyer seeing the "bones" of your home. A large Christmas tree placed strategically in front of a window can make it difficult for a prospective buyer to look at your view. Oversize decorations can make even a large room feel small, and can overwhelm a small room. Lights taped into a window can be distracting at best, and downright dangerous if you've overloaded a circuit. Outside, a full-blown lighting display can hide elegant features of your home's exterior.

And whatever religion you practice, there's bound to be someone who follows a different religion who will tour your home while it is listed. While your decorations aren't designed to offend anyone, they could make a buyer feel she'll never really be at home in your house. So keep all holiday decorations to a minimum. It'll certainly make it easier to clean up after the holidays are over.

Family Artwork

Every parent I know has a child who is a budding Picasso, or Monet, or Matisse—well, you get the picture. When our children bring home their work from school, they often ask us to display it on the refrigerator. Or the walls, windows, hallways—just about anywhere a piece of paper will hang.

While I do believe it is important to validate and encourage your child's artistic impulses, it's not as important as getting your house sold. (And, of course, once you're in your new home, you can go back to putting up their artwork everywhere.) While you're limiting your holiday decorations, put a moratorium on displaying your children's artwork until you have accepted an offer. And that includes limiting the displays on the refrigerator, as well as on the windows, the walls, and the doors.

Invitations, Phone Lists, School Calendars, and Other Important Pieces of Paper

Every family accumulates a mass of party invitations, phone lists, school calendars, and notes about snack days and field trips, among other items. Typically, this stuff ends up clipped to magnets attached to the refrigerator door. Or there's a corkboard with an ever-changing mosaic of family information.

Before you list your home, pare down the paperwork to a minimum, and make sure you're keeping the refrigerator and other vertical surfaces as neat and clean as possible.

A GOOD START

When it comes to holiday decorations, make do with less both inside and outside your house. Limit yourself by time and by the amount of stuff you put up.

- **Time.** The trouble with holidays isn't that they last too long; just the opposite. We try to extend our holiday feelings by stretching the days we celebrate. Try to limit the amount of time your decorations are up when selling your home. You might want to put up your tree a week before Christmas and bring it down on New Year's Day (the two-week period when only *serious* shoppers are out looking for homes). If you're Jewish, limit Hanukkah decorations to the actual eight days the holiday is celebrated. If you celebrate Kwanza, keep decorations just for the seven days the holiday is celebrated.

- **Quantity.** Don't go all out during the winter holidays. Limit yourself to one tree per house, or one menorah per person, instead of filling the entire house with holiday clutter and memorabilia. Keep your exterior lighting displays simple and elegant.

School and Artwork

Create a special box for each child's art or schoolwork. Take down the artwork from your walls and refrigerator, and allow your children to choose which piece gets saved and stored away and which gets dumped. Store the boxes in an easily accessible place so you can look often at projects, memorabilia, and other homemade treasures.

Remember, Decorations Distract Buyers

Resist the temptation to overdecorate your home for the many other holidays and special days during the year. Every decoration you put up could affect a buyer's opinion of your home. This takes his or her mind off the main goal of buying your home. Worse, it could make a buyer forget what your home looks like—instead, they'll just remember the lovely decorations.

8

Timing Is Everything: Making the Right Marketing Moves

HAVE A PRELISTING INSPECTION

Home buyers have become much more sophisticated over the past dozen years. In some ways, that makes the job of selling your home a little more difficult. For example, years ago, far fewer home buyers spent the money on a professional home inspection. Today, nearly everyone has the home they intend to buy professionally inspected. But growing consumer reliance on professional home inspectors has forced states to take a second look at regulating the industry. Currently, only a few states, including Illinois and Texas, regulate professional home inspectors, but the odds are high that more states will require inspectors to take exams and get a state license in the near future.

The point of having a home inspection is to learn what problems or physical issues a home may have, and what it might cost to fix them. Because many sellers don't often recognize that their home is flawed, they don't regard that as problematic for buyers. They don't realize they need to fix these defects until the buyer—having read the inspection report—requests it. How bad can the situation get? A perfectly normal house deal can quickly turn ugly if a buyer decides to exercise his or her right to terminate the deal based on an unsatisfactory inspection report. On the other hand, the inspection might turn up one or two serious issues—like, there is gas leaking from the hot-water heater—and a few minor ones, such as broken windowpanes, ripped screens, and loose doorknobs. These problems—even the "serious" gas-leaking issue—can be easily resolved by a seller willing to fix the problems or reduce the purchase price so that the buyer can get the issues resolved. But if the inspection report turns up asbestos, and the seller refuses to pay to have it removed, the buyer may toss up his or her hands and walk away from the deal.

Mold is one of the big issues of the day for home buyers. When Robin and Tim were looking for a house to buy, they fell in love with a two-story forty-year-old home that was vacant. Unfortunately, the seller had turned off the heating and air-conditioning to the house, and Robin and Tim's inspector found that much of the house was covered in mold. Could this problem be fixed? Maybe. But it would have meant ripping off and replacing most of the plasterboard (also known as drywall) in the house. It would have taken a lot of time, not to mention money, and the sellers were in the middle of a bad divorce. Robin and Tim chose to give up the house and find another.

To get on top of the game, many sellers are now paying their own home inspectors to do a *prelisting inspection*. Essentially, a prelisting inspection is a professional home inspection, except that the seller pays for it, and it typically occurs well before any home buyers step across your threshold. It may even happen before you've hired your agent.

What is a home inspector looking for in a prelisting inspection? Anything that an inspector would point out to a prospective buyer: warped floors, cracks in walls and floors, signs of water problems, problems with the mechanical systems, and failing roof shingles. The inspector may point out items that should be fixed (like a broken window sash), replaced (cracked shower door), or removed (the stack of boxes hiding the crack in the foundation).

Of course, what you do with the report you receive from your inspector is up to you. Most agents would advise you to fix most of the items that have been flagged—especially all the major ones. That's because you'll likely see these very same items again in the buyer's home inspection report. At that time, if the defects haven't been dealt with, the buyer will use the list to renegotiate the price of the property.

Of course, you'll have the right to refuse to negotiate, but inspection report items have been known to sour many a home sale. Your best bet is to hire the best home inspector you can find to do a prelisting inspection and act on the results before you put your house on the market.

You May Have to Disclose

The only concern you should have about a prelisting inspection is the possibility that something big will turn up that you can't fix without spending a lot of money. If it does, you'll have two options:

- **Fix the problem.** You always have the option of fixing whatever problem you've discovered. And, as long as the problem isn't huge, you should be able to take care of it in a timely manner. For example, if the inspector discovers that you have a cracked heat exchange in your furnace, you'd want to know that. Then you can have a heating expert come in to replace the furnace. If you're in a neighborhood popular with FHA or VA buyers, you'll need to bring your home up to code before the deal can close, so fixing the problem is probably the best course of action. Your home inspector should be up-to-date on current FHA and VA code requirements, but you should ask if this is the case when you call.

- **Disclose the issue.** Now that you know the problem exists, you generally must disclose it to a buyer. Let's say the inspector finds that you have a serious termite problem. You can fix the problem, but you may have to disclose it on your seller disclosure form (depending on what your state law says). In many states, seller disclosure law requires you to disclose a material defect that cannot be seen. If the inspector calls such a defect to your attention, and you have not repaired the problem, you may now be required to tell the buyer about it. Your real-estate agent should have a copy of your state's seller disclosure requirements, or you can call your state's real-estate commission and find out what kind of disclosure you're required to make.

Of course, you can always do nothing—but that won't help you sell your house faster and for more money.

A GOOD START

Every good real-estate agent has a list of home inspectors he or she likes. Ask your agent to recommend two or three inspectors for a prelisting inspection. If you haven't hired a real-estate agent yet, call the agent who sold you your property, or you can log onto the Web site of the American Society of Home Inspectors (www.ASHI.org.) to find a list of ASHI-certified inspectors near you. If you own a home with a synthetic-stucco coating, you'll want an inspector who has been trained in problems and issues associated with these products.

Other problems may require you to hire a specialist. You can hire a company that will test your home for radon (a colorless, odorless gas that can cause serious damage, particularly in young children), termites and other pests, problems with septic systems, and lead. If you suspect your house has any of these problems, you may want to hire a specialist to do further testing before you list your home. Expect to pay at least $200 for each test. You can ask your home inspector for recommendations, but be wary if you are referred to a company that is tied somehow to your inspector. You may also be able to get names from your real-estate attorney or agent.

Don't be afraid to ask friends and family members for recommendations of home inspectors, contractors, or specialists with whom they had a good experience. Once you have your handful of names, you can begin the interviewing process. Here's what to do when you call the inspectors:

- **Compare fees.** Fees vary widely. Some inspectors charge by the size of your home, others by the sales price. Some charge a flat fee, and synthetic-stucco inspectors charge more than anyone else. Expect to spend $250 to $600 on your prelisting inspection, comparable to what a home buyer would pay.

- **Ask what's included in the fee and how long the inspection will take.** Expect to spend at least two hours for a thorough interior and exterior inspection of your property.

- **Compare telephone manners.** The inspector should be courteous and knowledgeable.

- **Ask if the inspector is licensed, bonded, and insured.** Ask if the inspector guarantees his or her performance. For example, if the inspector misses something major and the buyer's inspector finds out, you'll wind up in a less-effective negotiating position. But if your inspector had found out the problem in the prelisting inspection, you could have fixed the problem before anyone would have found out. Will the inspector refund the fee you paid if something he or she misses turns up on the buyer's inspection later?

- **Ask if the inspector is a current member of ASHI or another professional home inspection trade group.** Be sure to ask what the qualifications are for membership and exactly how many years' experience the inspector has. You can contact ASHI to find out if the inspector is a member in good standing.

- **Ask about written documentation.** Many of the best inspectors carry a handheld computer that automatically generates a written report. Others will take notes, go back to their office, and write up a report, which they fax to the client. You should end up with something in writing, and the report should contain more than checkmarks ("Good," "Average," "Below Average") on a form.

- **Ask for references—and then call them.** Ideally, you should talk to the last three or four people the inspector has worked for.

- **Ask how many inspections the inspector performs each year.** If the inspector has more than one inspection scheduled every three hours, it's probably not enough time (including travel time to each property) to do a thorough inspection. Condos typically take one to two hours each, depending on the size, and an inspection for a single-family house can last as long as three hours.

If you get the feeling over the phone that the inspector has other things he or she would rather be doing than talking to you, hang up and try another name. You want to hire the best person for the job, not the busiest.

CHECK OUT YOUR COMPETITION

Before you put your house on the market, it pays to do a little research. So check out the competition. It's easy to do—simply start by visiting open houses in your neighborhood.

Why do you want to find out about the other homes on the market? It's important to develop a mental inventory of what's been sold and what is currently available for sale. You're looking to see what condition the homes are in, what amenities they have, and how much the owners are asking. Then you should to compare these homes to your own. Ask yourself the following questions:

1. Is my home bigger or smaller than this property? Size matters to home buyers. If your condo, co-op, town home, or single-family house is bigger than your neighbor's, and both you and your neighbor are asking the same amount of money for the property, your home may be perceived as a better deal because it offers more square feet for the money.

2. Is my home in better or worse shape? These days, condition may be the single most important reason why your house will or won't sell. Price is important, but often a buyer will pay a little extra for a house that's in "blue ribbon" or "move-in" condition. After spending as much as they can to buy your home, most buyers don't have much left to spend on improvements. So even if your house is bigger than your neighbor's, if it's in far worse condition, you may have a problem getting the same price.

3. What amenities do competitive houses have that mine doesn't? Let's imagine that you live in a subdivision of identical homes. But yours has fancier tile (marble instead of ceramic), stainless-steel kitchen appliances (instead of white or beige), and a higher quality of carpet or even hardwood floors. All other things being equal, you should be able to command a slightly higher price than your neighbor because of your upgrades. Remember, no two existing homes are really equal, even in a sea of "identical town houses," because people decorate and live differently (for better or worse) in their homes. So when counting amenities, don't just include the upgrades, but also the number of rooms and bathrooms, garden and landscaping, and the condition.

4. How does each house, condo, or town house compare with others in the neighborhood that are for sale? Collect listing sheets from all the open houses you visit, and make notes about how each house measures up in size, condition, and amenities.

By comparing the size, condition, and amenities of each house with the listing price and, ultimately, the sales price, you should get an excellent idea of how much homes are selling for and what the true market value of your own home is.

And true market value is what you're after when you're selling your home. It's an excellent idea to price your home just above its market value. (In a seller's market, you'll price it a bit higher above market value; in a buyer's market, you'll price it a bit lower. See Step 43 for more information on pricing your home correctly.) If you're realistic in the listing price you set, based on the size, condition, and amenities your property offers, you should have many more prospective buyers walk through your door.

A GOOD START

When you visit these other homes for sale in the neighborhood, you're trying to develop a body of knowledge of what true value is for property at that point in time. Of course, true value shifts constantly in real estate, and it's impossible to stay 100 percent current with market values, but the idea is to have a general sense of what things cost and what people are getting for their money.

To deepen your knowledge, take a camera with you to the open houses. (A digital camera works well because it's pretty quiet, but a Polaroid camera is fine, too, or you can buy cheap, disposable cameras at the drugstore and always keep one in the glove compartment of your car.) You want to have a camera so that you can document the specific amenities you find in a house.

Print your photographs, separate them by house, and clip them to the listing sheet for that property. Three-hole punch the listing sheets, and insert them in a three-ring binder (or just keep them in a manila folder you can get at easily). As the homes get sold, you'll want to go back and jot down the price the buyers paid for the properties. You can find out the sales prices by asking your agent to look them up for you, or by going to the office of the recorder of deeds in your area (you'll likely find them at your county hall) and looking up the sales data. Many newspapers also publish recent sales prices, so check out the real-estate section of your local paper for useful, but often delayed, data.

You might also want to note how long it takes to sell each home that's listed in your neighborhood. It's one thing if a house sells for its list price in a day. It's quite another if a house take several months to sell, and the owner only gets 91 percent of the asking price. How long a property stays on the market tells you a great deal about where the housing market is in your neighborhood.

USE TECHNOLOGY TO ITS BEST ADVANTAGE

When I wrote my last book on selling your home (*100 Questions Every Home Seller Should Ask*), the Internet, as we know it, was only a few years old. Young start-up tech companies were just discovering the real-estate world, with its antiquated ways of doing business. Since 1995, the Internet and computer technology have begun to seriously change the way we purchase and sell our homes. In fact, 75 percent of all home buyers start their search on the Internet.

That number is increasing every year, which means that if you want to boost your profits when you sell your home, you must make the best use of technology and the Web.

There is an enormous amount of technology and software—not to mention an estimated one million real-estate Web sites—that can help you sell your home faster and for more money. Below are some of the most important high-tech aids you should be able to use.

The Internet

Here's how you would have sold your home before we had superfast computers and the Internet: You'd list your home with an agent, and once a week, the agent's database would generate a "hot sheet" listing all the new homes for sale that week. Twice a month, listings would be printed in a book as big as a telephone book, except it would have had a pale pink, yellow, or beige paper cover, depending on the state. These listing books were jealously guarded by real-estate agents, and neither buyers nor sellers were allowed to peruse the books except in the company of their agent. (If you were really lucky, and the agent didn't mind breaking a few rules, you might have been able to take an old one home overnight.)

What a difference a few bytes make. Today, technology is redefining how we shop for, analyze, communicate about, finance, list, buy, and sell our homes. If you're selling your home, and you don't use the Internet, there's no guarantee you'll get the best deal.

That's because when you use the Internet to get the word out about selling your home, prospective buyers (and their friends and family) all over the world can tune in and see what you have for sale. If you're selling by owner—that is, without the assistance of a full-service agent or discount broker—the Internet provides a relatively inexpensive way to advertise your house. You can either list your home on any number of FSBO Web sites or by setting up a home page that vibrantly shows off all the amenities associated with your home. But the Internet also offers other options, including listing your home for sale on eBay (and conducting a sale via auction). The Internet's real-estate functionality is increasing each year, and it's not that difficult to look into a crystal ball and see streaming video of homes for sale and electronic closings in our future. (For a few different FSBO and discount brokerage Web sites you might want to try, turn to "A Good Start," located at the end of this section.)

If you list with an agent, your listing will not only appear on the agent's personal Web site, but will also be uploaded to sites that drive millions of visitors a month, like Realtor.com and HomeAdvisor.com. If your agent's company belongs to a franchise, like Century 21, Coldwell Banker, RE/MAX, or ERA, your listing will also appear on the franchise's main site.

Digital Photos

In the days of the old listing books, a photographer would come to your home and take what became a very grainy, black-and-white photo of the exterior of your home. If you lived in a condo, the photographer would shoot the exterior of the building. Hardly the best way to show the true nature of a property.

With the Internet, you can use crystal-clear, color digital photos that can be increased to full-screen size with the click of a mouse. You also can access 360-degree photos that allow a viewer to feel as though he is standing inside a room and turning in a circle to see the entire space. You see everything in that room, in living color.

Some Web sites already contain video of a particular home or room, and T 1 lines allow you to stream video, though not many sellers have access to or can make the best use of the technology. As technology and bandwidth increases, you'll be able to show home movies of your house.

E-Scheduling

If someone wants to see your home, he or she can call your agent and ask for a showing. Or buyers can call their broker, who then calls your agent to schedule a showing. The listing agent is in charge of the schedule.

But that's starting to change, thanks to the development of scheduling software. What this software does is put the schedule of showings for your home on a secured Web site. You, or a buyer, can log on at any time and actually see what showings are scheduled for and when. As the seller, you'll be able to electronically block out certain times so that no showings are scheduled.

The beauty of this system is that it allows everyone to communicate without spending a lot of time on the telephone. As the seller, you'll control when people come to see your home. The software shields the name of the person who is coming for a showing, so anonymity is preserved. Everyone can log on at any time to see what the schedule looks like, so it's very convenient. Without a doubt, you'll be seeing scheduling software grow in popularity over the next decade.

E-Mail

For some reason, real-estate agents have been slow (as a group) to adopt new technology. There's a sense from the real-estate industry that technology will take control of the deal away from agents, and perhaps that is why some agents refuse to make use of new technology developments.

But of all the new technology available to agents, electronic mail has become one of the few things the industry has embraced. Buyers and sellers use e-mail in their normal workday lives, and they expect their agents to communicate this way, as well. Unfortunately, many don't. One problem for agents with e-mail is that they're out of the office most of the time looking at properties. Now that handheld wireless computers are easier and cheaper to use, it's likely that agents will start to use e-mail to its fullest capacity.

Encrypted Key Cards

A lockbox is literally a box that locks up your home. If an agent has the right code, or a special key card, he or she can open the box and take out the key to your home, open it up, and show it to a prospective buyer.

Sounds great, but if you allow your agent to put a lockbox on your home, you're essentially giving the agent permission to let the buyer and the buyer's agent walk around your home unescorted. I don't think this helps sell your home for the most money. I think it's an easier way for seller's agents to take a lot of listings without doing the work they should to show all these homes to their best advantage.

I think, and in some places this is quite controversial, you should insist that your agent personally show your home. Why? Because next to you, no one knows your home better than the agent who is listing it for sale. But in the event that you do permit a lockbox to be installed on your front door, the buyer's agent should have some sort of smart or encrypted key card that would open the door. (In some areas, it's a key, but this practice is quickly being replaced.)

With a smart card, the lockbox keeps track of which agent has entered your house, the time it was entered, and the time the agent left. If something was out of order, or if something was found to be missing during the time the box identified the agent as being there, you would know who to talk to.

A GOOD START

Whether you're selling on your own or using an agent, you should consider creating an inexpensive Web site for your property. You can purchase a domain name for $35 per year (or less), and buy the cheapest hosting package from any of a number of hosting sites (which will cost as little as a few hundred dollars per year). Microsoft FrontPage is one of several easy Web site creation programs that anyone can use (if you already know how to use Microsoft Word, you're ahead of the game). In fact, some of the Web-hosting sites will automatically create Web pages for you—for free. You'll want to upload digital photos, perhaps a map showing where the property is located, the price, and contact information. Once you have your site, you'll want to list it with the top search engines.

(Start your search for a site at any Internet name registration site. You can find a listing of Accredited Registrar Sites at www.Internic.com, and then click through to any of the thousands of sites that register domain names. The price of a domain name is currently $35 per year, or less—if the site underwrites part of the U.S. registration fee with the hopes that you'll use its Web-site package services. Just remember, you won't need this site for long, so don't sign up for any services for longer than a year. In fact, paying monthly, if you can, is preferable. When your agent is putting together marketing materials, make sure he or she includes the name of your property's Web site.)

The next step is to get the word out. While it's fun to think that someone across the country or from another continent is going to buy your home, it's likely going to be someone who already lives close by or who knows someone who lives close by. Create a flyer (decidedly low tech) that has your Web address on it, and pass it out in your neighborhood. Slip it under doors, in mailboxes, or under the windshield wipers of cars parked on your street. Make use of free bulletin boards that some local retailers will make available to you, such as the grocery store, the dry cleaners, or the beauty shop. Hire your children and their friends to pass out flyers on the street in front of your house along with lemonade or hot chocolate. Put your Web address on the "for sale" sign in your front yard. Send an e-mail to your friends, family, and associates with the Web address attached. Ask them to forward the Web address to any interested parties.

There are other technologies that are currently being developed that will help buyers and sellers. Be aware that some agents are more tech-savvy than others, but that doesn't necessarily make them a better choice. There are a lot of reasons to choose an agent, and technology is only one facet of the agent experience. How do you choose an agent who's tech-savvy? You have to spend time with the agent, talking about technology. If you choose someone who uses some or all of the technologies I've described, it's likely the agent and his or her firm will be on the cutting edge, and will adopt new technology as it becomes available. These tools make the home-buying or -selling process easier, faster, or more profitable for everyone.

SIMPLE STEP
36

INTERVIEW SEVERAL AGENTS BEFORE YOU HIRE ONE

If you've never sold a home before, you may be unaware of how different the process is from buying. When you sell a home, most of the work you do occurs before you list it:

- Cleaning up and making it shine.

- Doing market research.

- Hiring the right broker.

- Setting the right price.

Then you wait—sometimes less than patiently. When you buy a home, most of the work happens after you hire the agent. That's when you tour properties, do market research, find a mortgage, make an offer, and so forth.

For buyers and sellers, the process of hiring the right agent hasn't changed much in decades. You want to hire someone who is extremely knowledgeable about the housing stock in your neighborhood, who has worked full-time and logged a number of years in the residential real-estate business, and who knows the agents representing the buyers and other sellers in your neighborhood. Anyone without these qualifications simply won't do.

So, how do you find the right agent? Start by interviewing at least three people from three different firms. For variety's sake, you might try an agent from a large national firm (like Century 21, Coldwell Banker, RE/MAX, or ERA), an agent from a large local firm, and an agent from a small neighborhood firm. Each of these types of companies has pluses and minuses.

Big firms tend to have a lot of resources, a lot of technology, and a lot going on. Your agent might have one or two assistants, and after the first meeting, you might work exclusively with them. But if you have a home that requires specialized marketing, or if you want to cut a different sort of deal, the huge real-estate chains have, to some degree, tied the hands of their agents on the local level with respect to marketing and advertising, as well as other issues. Large local firms have some of the same resources as a large national firm, but they have more of a local presence, which is a good thing. But you could easily find yourself and your listing lost in the shuffle of a big firm. Small neighborhood real-estate firms intimately know the neighborhoods, but often lack the resources of a big firm. Still, there are neighborhoods where the top firm is the mom-and-pop shop, not one of the big players.

Which size firm is best? It depends. You'll want to go with the firm that employs the agent that's right for your home. Here are some tips for gathering together a shortlist of names of agents who might be able to help you sell:

- **Check "for sale" signs:** Which agents have signs posted most frequently in your neighborhood? Which agents regularly sell homes most quickly in your neighborhood?

- **Go to open houses:** Talk to the agent who is listing the property. Do you keep seeing the same agents hosting different open houses?

- **Check out the real-estate section in your local newspaper:** Which agents are advertising the houses that are for sale in your neighborhood? How frequently do they advertise a particular home?

- **Ask around:** Talk to family members, friends, neighbors, and coworkers about who they used to buy or sell and if they had a good (or great) experience. Don't take a recommendation unless the buyer or seller had a good or great experience.

After Pam's mother died, she decided to sell her home. She talked to her friends and relatives about who they had used to sell their homes in the neighborhood. One of Pam's cousins passed along the name of an agent she had used. Pam called her and ended up hiring her. What a mistake! The agent was just horrible, and Pam, who never says an unkind word about anyone, could hardly contain herself. She ended up firing the agent and hiring another, who got her mother's home sold. Months later, she ran into this cousin and asked her whether she had enjoyed working with the agent.

"Oh, no," Pam's cousin replied. "She was horrible."

"So, why did you give her name to me?" Pam asked.

"Well," the cousin replied, "you said you wanted a name. I gave you the only one I had."

Once you have a shortlist of two or three names, invite each agent over to tour your home and do a comparative marketing analysis (CMA). A CMA is essentially a sales proposal that the agent uses to solicit your listing. A good CMA contains several important pieces of information:

- **Comps.** "Comps" are the sales prices of homes, comparable to yours in size, shape, and amenities, that have recently sold in your neighborhood. Agents use comps to determine how much your home is really worth.

- **Suggested listing price.** After analyzing the data and viewing your home, agents will come up with a suggested list price. What I've found is that if you invite three different agents to tour the same property and ask each to prepare a CMA, you'll end up with three different prices. Typically, one will be higher, one lower, and one in the middle. But because life isn't the Goldilocks story, you can't say one of the three prices is going to be right. So don't rule anyone out based on the suggested list price that agent comes up with. If you like the agent but don't think he or she is right on the price, you can hire him or her anyway and decide together on what will be the right list price for your home.

- **Marketing strategy.** This is the place in the sales proposal where the agent tells you what he or she is going to do to get the word out about your property. The agent should talk to you about technology, Web sites, advertising, and open houses for brokers and buyers.

A GOOD START

Here's how the CMA process works: You invite each agent over separately to tour your home. Remember, your home should already be in fabulous shape, but while each agent is touring your home, ask him or her if there is anything you could do that would increase the sales price or make the home sell faster. A good agent should give you as much advice as possible. Beware of an agent who seems to be skimping on the advice or holding back information with promises that you'll get the "full treatment" once you sign the listing agreement, because that could lead to the unpleasant discovery that the agent in fact had no tricks up her sleeve.

The agent will then leave your home and call you a day or so later when the CMA is completed. Typically, the agent comes to your home to present his or her findings and walk you through the proposal. At this point, you should interview the agent. Ask the following questions:

- How long have you been an agent?
- How many sellers do you work with in a year?

- How many buyers do you work with?
- How many of your homes sell to first-time buyers?
- How many are priced in the midrange or are in the upper brackets?
- What are the prices of first-time-buyer homes, midrange homes, and upper-bracket homes in this area?
- Do you work full-time?
- How long have you worked for your firm?
- Do you expect to take any vacations in the near future? How long will you be gone?
- Do you have some references that I can call? (If you take reference numbers, be sure to call them. And again, make sure that the references had a superlative experience with the agent.)

After you've been presented with each CMA, take some time to think about which agent you liked the best, and which proposal you feel is best tailored to you and your home. Was there one agent with whom you felt a particular connection?

Remember, working with an agent on a sale or purchase is like being in a short-term "marriage." You have to have good communication, or the process will be frustrating from start to finish.

Usually, after going through the CMA process, one agent will stand out. If this doesn't happen, you have a couple of choices: Ask a fourth agent to come in and present a CMA, or start a whole new round by inviting three new agents in to create and present a CMA.

CONSIDER USING A DISCOUNT BROKER OR SELLING BY OWNER

The extraordinary seller's market that began around 1994 produced two new surprises: The number of FSBOs (a commonly used acronym for the term *for sale by owner*—that is, people selling their homes themselves without the help of an agent) began to rise, and discount brokers began to emerge as a possible alternative for sellers who felt they needed to list their homes in the local MLS to stay competitive, but wanted to do more on their own and pay less in commission.

Should You Sell by Owner?

The National Association of Realtors is a powerful lobbying force in Washington, D.C., and the trade organization to which about 700,000 agents, roughly half the agents in the United States, belong. (An agent who is a member of the NAR is called a Realtor.) According to the NAR, the proportion of people selling homes without agents is about 15 percent over the past few decades.

But many real-estate-industry observers think the actual number of FSBOs is higher than that—perhaps as high as 25 to 30 percent—depending on where the house is located. Anecdotally, many people know of neighbors who sold by owner and ended up with bidding wars. In some hot urban neighborhoods during the late 1990s, as many as 50 percent of owners were selling by owner. Of course, there's no official way to calculate how many sellers are doing without the services of a full-service real-estate-brokerage firm. But you should know that plenty of people can, and do, sell their homes without paying a broker's commission.

The real question is this: *Should* you sell your home yourself? Not paying 5 to 7 percent commission (the average commission in the United States is now down to about 5.5 percent, according to statistics from the NAR) sounds wonderful. On every $100,000 of sales price you'll save about $5,500. That's a hefty chunk of change. And you'll control who has access to your home.

But selling on your own is extremely challenging. I've sold by owner, paying a half commission to the broker who brought the buyer. I've also bought by owner. When we first saw the house in which we now live, it was listed, but we couldn't come to terms. A few months later, we drove by again, but the house was off the market. I knocked on the door, and it turned out the owner was now ready to sell and move. (The seller ended up paying a partial commission to his agent anyway, a longtime friend.)

Selling by owner can be tough on you and your family. You should only consider selling by owner if you have the time and patience to get through it with a smile on your face. Why? Being a seller is daunting enough. (You have to keep your home sparklingly clean, get ready to pick up the family and leave at a moment's notice when a prospective buyer calls, and keep up on your market research.) Tacking on the real-estate agent's job while you're working and perhaps parenting is a fair amount of extra work—even if the financial rewards are worth it.

In addition to your job as a seller, FSBO means you must also take on the marketing and showing of your home. Bear in mind that most sellers talk too much—if they get a buyer inside the threshold, they end up chatting endlessly about the condition of the home, and all of its wonderful amenities. While it's important to point some things out, people know what each room is, and they know how light switches work. So let buyers in the door, and then allow them to walk through and "experience" your home without too much interference from you.

If you do decide to sell your own home, make sure you're ready now, before you list your property:

- **Know what your property is worth.** Even if you don't intend to use an agent, go through the CMA process described in Step 36. Most agents will be delighted to help you because they know only a small percentage of FSBOs sell without the help of a brokerage firm. This is their opportunity to market their services to you. A CMA will give you an excellent sense of what your property is worth. If you rely only on Web sites like Domania.com (which lists some of the sales prices of comparable homes in your area, but not all), you'll be looking through incomplete, old data that will not be as reliable or as accurate as the data real-estate agents can pull up from the MLS.

- **Don't be greedy.** Don't think that because you're not using an agent you'll pocket the entire commission. It doesn't work that way. Buyers who purchase without an agent expect to share some of your savings. Or they may bring a buyer's agent with them and ask you to pay a half commission. Even if you pay a half commission, this still represents an enormous savings of 2.5 to 3.5 percent out of the standard 5 to 7 percent total sales commission you'd pay to a full-service firm, and you should find a way to work out the deal.

- **Make your property available.** You can't sell by owner if you don't have the time to be there when people want to see your home. If you make yourself available only on Saturdays and Sundays, you'll wait a long time until the right buyer comes along.

- **Don't show your property by yourself.** For safety's sake, have another person in the house. Frequently, con artists posing as home buyers will come through, and one person will try to distract you while the other "buyer" robs you (see Step 14). There have been reports in southern California of female real-estate agents in some of the beach towns being raped while hosting open houses. In Chicago a few years ago, a real-estate agent was killed while hosting an open house. You don't want something unfortunate happening while you're trying to sell your own home, so make sure someone else is around, particularly if you hold an open house.

- **Use an attorney to prepare your contract and close your deal.** This is especially important if you're in a state like California, Ohio, or Georgia, where attorneys aren't commonly used because real-estate agents control all aspects of the deal. If you don't use an attorney and you don't use an agent, you may not know what specific disclosures your state requires, and you won't know how to complete the closing process. For tips on how to find a qualified real-estate attorney, see Step 46.

- **Be prepared to qualify every buyer.** You will want every buyer to be a "cash" buyer. That is, either the buyer is going to pay in cash, or there's no mortgage contingency (a rider to the contract that permits the buyer to back out of the deal if he or she can't get financing on reasonable terms). How do you get around the mortgage contingency? If the buyer has been preapproved for his mortgage, he should have a letter from his lender, committing in writing to fund the loan provided the house appraises out in value. (An independent appraiser confirms the value of the house by comparing it to other homes recently sold.) You may also want to ask the buyer to provide you with a copy of his preapproval letter from the lender.

Discount Brokers

Being a discount broker wasn't something agents often bragged about—and in some parts of the country, it's still that way. Discount brokers allow you to do some of the work yourself when it comes to selling a home, and you save a chunk of the commission.

Mostly, discount brokers list your property on the local MLS and give you a sign to put up on your front lawn. The rest is up to you. While some will help you do a little more, you may pay for each telephone call or showing. Those costs can mount fast, especially if you're paying $20 for each telephone call, $10 for a fax, and so on.

Ideally, you want your home to be listed on the MLS and a few different Web sites. You also need a sign for your front lawn. Naturally, you want to pay as little as possible for these services. There are discount firms that charge $499 for the MLS listing plus another $150 for a virtual tour of your house that will get posted on various Web sites. If you can sell this way, you'll save yourself thousands of dollars.

And plenty of people do sell this way. Monica had her house listed for $360,000 with a full-service agent and received an offer for nearly the full price the first day. She had agreed to pay her agent a 6 percent commission, and quickly realized that she'd pay $21,000 in commission. She asked her agent to reduce her commission, since she didn't have to work very hard to get the sale, but the agent refused. So Monica didn't accept the offer, and refused to counter.

When the listing agreement expired, Monica listed with a discount agent that charged her $499 for the MLS listing plus an extra $100 for digital photos. Within a week she had an offer for the same amount she had previously declined and saved about $20,000 in commission.

Of course, the time to do the math is *before* you sign your listing agreement. The full-service agent would probably say that Monica had paid for the agent's expertise in setting the right price and doing the right kind of marketing. Some deals are easy and some are hard, the agent might say. But why should you pay more for an easy deal if you can do it yourself? Remember, just because you got an offer quickly the first time doesn't mean you'll get another one several months later. Real-estate markets change frequently, and when you sell your own home, you take the very real risk that you won't do the right kind of marketing demanded by the local housing climate.

A GOOD START

The best time to sell your own home or use a discount agency is when your local neighborhood has become a seller's market. A seller's market is defined as a time when there are more buyers than homes available to purchase. It's possible for pockets of neighborhoods to be strong, while others are slumping. For example, as I was writing this book, a couple of neighborhoods near mine in the Chicago area were having a huge seller's market for homes priced under $300,000. Any time a house came up for that price or less, it was immediately snapped up by a developer, who tore down the house. The market for homes that cost up to $800,000 was also strong. But the market for superexpensive homes costing $1.2 million or more had slowed down tremendously. Depending on which kind of property you are marketing, you might try to sell by owner, or get a full-service agent.

If you're interested in exploring the discount brokerage market, you should know that only a few discount brokers operate nationally. Because real estate is a very local business, there are usually discount agents who will work in your area. The trick is to find them.

Below are some Web sites to start your search. I don't endorse any of these sites specifically, but they're a place to learn about what's available online. You should also check out IRED.com (the International Real Estate Digest) for additional FSBO and discount-broker listings. Before you sign any agreement, be sure to compare how much you'll pay with what you'll get, and check with the Better Business Bureau (www.bbb.org) to see if any complaints have been filed against the company.

FSBO Sites

EBay.com (auctions for homes and time-shares)

Forsalebyowner.com

FSBO.com

Owners.com

Discount Brokerage Sites

Listlow.com

HomeBytes.com

Listforless.com

Ziprealty.com

Ehomes.com

À La Carte Service

Offering buyers and sellers the opportunity to purchase some services is referred to as the "unbundling" of real-estate services. The big franchise companies like Coldwell Banker and Century 21 have been experimenting with allowing sellers to cherry-pick the services they need and pay less commission overall.

Under current law, all commissions are negotiable. If you feel that you're not completely prepared to take on the job of a FSBO, you can ask your full-service agent to do the job for less. It's unlikely you'll get anyone to take on your property for less than a 5 percent commission, but it's not unheard of. See Step 38 for ideas on how to creatively negotiate your commission and other "junk fees."

SIMPLE STEP
38

NEGOTIATE YOUR LISTING AGREEMENT

The listing agreement is one of the two most important documents you'll sign when you sell your home—the other being the sales contract. It governs your relationship with your agent and with the brokerage firm he or she works for. So it's important that you pay attention to what the listing agreement says, and understand how you can revise it to better work for you.

Although the listing agreement is a valid, binding legal document, many sellers sign it without even reading it, which can lead to serious problems down the road. Before you sign a listing agreement, everything is negotiable. Once you've signed it, you're pretty much stuck with what's printed on the contract.

Here are the important issues you need to think about before you sign the listing agreement. You should modify any listing agreement to allow you to:

- **Take the property off the market.** How long will you list your home initially? I generally recommend that sellers should limit each listing period to ninety days, or roughly three months. While that seems like a long time, in a balanced market (where there are an equal number of buyers and sellers) it's about how long it should take for your property to sell. In a hot market, your home could be under contract within thirty days or less. In northern California, a house recently received eighteen offers on the first day it was listed and ultimately sold for $100,000 more than the asking price. But in a slow market, your home could take a long time to sell, perhaps even as long as a year.

If you sign a listing agreement for 180 days, or six months, the language of the contract might force you to keep the property active with this agent, even if you want to switch to another brokerage company or if circumstances change in your life. But you should retain the right to take the property off the market. If, for some reason, you decide to stay in your home, no one should have the right to force you to sell—or pay a commission if you're brought a full-price offer.

- **Switch brokers and not pay a double commission.** You can spend days, weeks, or even months interviewing brokers before selecting your listing agent. And despite all the care you take, your relationship with the listing agent might not work out.

  If that's the case, you want the right to find another broker and not owe the first agent a commission on the sale of your home. Brokerage firms know they won't get paid if you take away the listing. So, they'll try to convince you that you owe them for the work they did previously. Strike the relevant clause in the listing agreement, or you could wind up legally owing a double commission when you sell.

- **Pay the commission only out of the closing proceeds.** When preparing to take the state license exams, wanna-be agents and brokers are taught that they've "earned" a commission once they bring what's known as a "ready, willing, and able" buyer to the seller or an offer that the buyer finds acceptable. That translates into a full-price offer with no contingencies (riders and amendments added to the contract that allow the buyer to pull out of the deal if certain things don't happen). While it seems far-fetched to think you'll receive that kind of offer right off the bat, homes that are priced right often receive multiple bids and sell in excess of the list price.

But even if an offer has been received and accepted, many things can cause a sale to fail, which is why you don't want to pay the broker's commission up front. Strike any clause in the listing agreement that says you owe a commission if a "ready, willing, and able" buyer is found. Add a clause to the agreement that states that the broker will get paid only upon the closing of the sale of your home and from the proceeds of the sale.

- **Terminate the agreement.** There are several reasons why you might want to cancel your listing agreement with a brokerage firm: You might have a personality conflict with the agent, or you might disagree over marketing strategies, the list price, or whether the agent is actually doing his or her job well.

  Rob thought his broker was doing a terrible job. He was always on vacation, and the other brokers in the office didn't know the property and didn't want to pick up the slack for Rob's broker. So they lied to Rob about the true level of interest in the property, didn't show the property, and let prospective buyers slip away. When Rob found out about all the deceit, he tried to get out of the listing agreement, but the firm wouldn't agree. Not wanting to run up a huge legal bill, Rob stuck it out, and then later complained to the agency that regulates real-estate agents and brokerage firms in his state.

  Whatever the case, you must retain the right to terminate the listing agreement. As with any legal agreement, you should terminate the agreement in writing, either by fax, mail, overnight delivery, or messenger. The best way to deliver notice is by certified mail, return receipt requested. You can do so via fax, but you will want to follow up with certified mail or a hand-delivered letter with a receipt that is signed upon delivery. You probably don't want to give notice by e-mail, since the other party could claim it never arrived, and it could be difficult and expensive to prove receipt.

  Consider giving the agent five business days' or two weeks' notice to wrap up loose ends. But if you terminate for cause—if the broker has lied, stolen, or somehow cheated you—your contract should terminate immediately.

• **Not pay a commission six months after termination.** Let's say you list your home in October, and a nice couple comes to see you in February. But they don't offer enough money, and it's cold and snowy, and you don't feel like moving, anyway. So you pull your house off the market and terminate the listing agreement.

Three months later, the buyers knock at your door. In those three months, you've lost your job, had knee surgery, and have decided to live with your aging mother. Things have changed, the buyers are willing to offer a bit more money, and you've come down in price. You make a deal on the lawn and shake hands.

Everyone's happy except you because now you've gone back and looked at your listing agreement. It says you owe your broker a commission for up to six months after termination of the listing agreement if someone who saw the home when it was listed buys it in that six-month period.

Six months is a long time—and it's supposed to keep you from yanking your home off the market and immediately selling it to someone who saw it while it was listed, thereby stiffing your agent. You should try to reduce this six-month period to three or four months. While many firms won't accept that, some will, and it never hurts to ask.

A GOOD START

A listing agreement is a legal document, and you should always have your attorney look over legal documents before you sign them. I've given you the basic outline of what you should ask for to protect yourself. Your attorney can suggest modifications that should be made to your particular listing agreement. Even in states like Georgia and California, where home buyers and sellers don't usually use attorneys to close residential house deals, I think you should still hire an attorney and use him or her to protect you throughout the entire transaction.

If you opt to proceed without the assistance of an attorney, ask the agent to walk you through the listing agreement, point by point. If the legalese still seems difficult to understand, then have the agent explain it in clear layperson's English. Then write what the agent says at the side of the paragraph in question and have the agent initial it before you sign off. (In my book *100 Questions Every Home Seller Should Ask*, I walk you through all the documents needed to sell a home, including the listing agreement, the contract, and the seller-disclosure forms, and what each paragraph of the documents really means.)

Structuring the Commission

The agent's commission will usually be the single biggest cost you'll pay when you sell your home. Typically, sellers pay anywhere from 5 to 7 percent in commission—that's $5,000 to $7,000 for every $100,000 of sales price. According to the National Association of Realtors (NAR), the average commission a seller pays is around 5.5 percent.

No matter what is printed on the listing agreement, you should try to negotiate with the agent. If the agent says the commission is not negotiable, and refuses to talk about it, you should immediately think about hiring someone else. All commissions are negotiable, according to the Real Estate Settlement Procedures Act, also known as RESPA.

There are several ways you can negotiate the commission: You can ask to pay a straight 5 percent commission. Or you can suggest an escalating payment structure, such as paying

6 percent on the first $100,000, 5 percent on the next $400,000, and 4 percent thereafter, depending on how much your property is worth. Although it may seem unfair, sellers with the most expensive homes will have the biggest amount of leverage negotiating the commission. That's because a straight 4 percent commission on a $2 million house comes to $80,000. Even after you divide that between the two agents and the two brokerage firms, your agent will earn a commission of approximately $20,000 for selling the home. (It's a nice chunk of change, although more expensive houses require the agent to spend more money on marketing and promotion. The better agents receive a split greater than 50 percent of the commission their firms receive in the transaction.) You can also ask the agent what he or she can do for you in terms of lowering the commission. You should do this when the agent comes back to your home to present the comparative marketing analysis (CMA).

Of course, there are times when you might want to offer a higher commission. When? If you have a home that's going to be difficult to sell, and will require the agent to put in an extraordinary effort or would be expensive to create the custom marketing materials necessary to really do the job right, then you'd want to pay a higher commission. While that seems counterintuitive to saving money, you might very well be able to sell an expensive or difficult-to-sell home more quickly by raising the commission, which will ultimately lower your carrying costs (the cost of paying for and maintaining the property while you're waiting to sell it). That's because while no self-respecting broker would force her clients to buy a home simply because the commission is higher, the broker will make sure all clients will tour the home. (See Chapter 11 for more suggestions on what to do if a home isn't selling.)

Extra Fees and Referrals

You know that mortgage lenders often include "junk" fees, such as document preparation and underwriting fees, to pad their profit. Well, real-estate brokers have taken note and have added junk fees to the other closing costs a seller must pay. In other words, paying the commission is no longer enough. Now you have to pay fees for document preparation ($150 to $300 or more) and other miscellaneous charges such as a funding fee and closing-package fee.

You don't have to pay these junk fees. When you're negotiating the listing agreement, you can simply strike out the paragraph that states which fees the brokerage company will charge you. Or write in, "No fees beyond the commission will be charged." Many brokerage firms will remove the fees if you ask. Or the agent will pay for them out of his or her share of the commission. Either way, you shouldn't be paying them, unless someone can give you a very good reason why you should.

Finally, be aware that some listing agreements require you to use (or at least consider) the title company, the home inspector, the mortgage company, and other services owned by the brokerage firm your agent works for. I recommend you strike all that language. It's not up to the agent to tell you which companies to use. I've even seen listing agreements that compel the seller to use the services of an agent in the firm to buy his or her next property. Strike that, too. Again, you're the one with the cash. You should decide whom to use, not your seller's agent.

Of course, if the agent and brokerage firm provide excellent service, then go for it. You might have as good an experience buying your next home as you did selling this one. But never agree to it in advance, in writing.

SIMPLE STEP
39

BE CREATIVE WITH YOUR
OPEN HOUSES

Of the many tools a seller has at his or her disposal, few are as effective as an open house. An open house allows either agents or prospective buyers to walk through your home and take a look around without making a formal appointment.

Broker's open houses are typically held right after the property is listed. In some parts of the country, brokers' open houses are typically held on Tuesday or Thursday mornings. On one of the days, agents in the brokerage firm walk through the firms new listings so that they can preview properties for their clients. On the other day, agents from other firms are invited to come and walk through a property that has just been listed. On Saturdays and Sundays, open houses are traditionally held for prospective buyers in the area.

The traditional open houses are fine, but talk to your agent about ways you can spice up yours so that more interest will be generated in your property. For example, think about what would be the best time of day to have your open house. Some brokers hold open houses for home buyers during the week. For some people, it's easier to find time to drop by an early morning open house or a midweek early evening event than take up an entire Saturday or Sunday touring properties for sale.

When you hold a midweek open house (either in the early morning or around dinner time), it's nice to provide some sort of snack to stave off your visitors' hunger pains while they tour your home. (Brokers will nearly always provide some sort of snack and beverage at a broker's open house. In some areas, certain caterers are so popular that agents advertise that the catering would be done by so-and-so just to pull other agents in.)

A GOOD START

The time to talk about what kinds of open houses the agent feels would be appropriate for your home is when the agent or broker comes to your house to present the CMA. Inside the CMA, there should be a section on marketing your home, and open houses should be on the list.

I talked to my friend Lisa recently, and she said her agent had held only three open houses although her property had been on the market for nearly seven months. I asked Lisa if that seemed reasonable to her, and she said she had asked the broker to do more open houses, but the broker always said that homes don't sell at open houses, they sell through the MLS.

While being listed in the MLS does sell homes, open houses can also be extremely valuable. Open houses allow many buyers to walk through at one time. They allow agents and brokers to see what you've got, so that they can decide whether the property would meet the needs of any buyers they have.

When the agent comes to present a CMA, take the time to discuss his or her philosophy on open houses. Ask how many open houses the agent plans to hold initially (every other week for the first six weeks is excellent), and how often others will be planned if the home doesn't sell in that period of time. Talk about different kinds of open houses, like the midweek early morning or late-afternoon open houses, and what ideas might work in your neighborhood.

MAKE EVERYONE AWARE YOU ARE SELLING YOUR HOME

Once your home is listed, the first people who pass through the doors of your open house will probably be your neighbors. Sure, they're curious about how much you're asking for your home, and what amenities your house has. But they're probably also thinking about which of their friends or relatives might like the house and would want to move to the neighborhood.

Our communities are made stronger when friends and relatives move in. It helps make a neighborhood seem smaller and more connected—no small thing in this fast-paced world in which we live. Before you list your home, or shortly thereafter, you should enlist your neighbors' help in finding a buyer for your property. They can be the best source of marketing for your property because they already like living in the neighborhood. (And neighborhood passion is catching.)

Even though you've hired an agent, plan on spending a good deal of time letting everyone you know (and everyone *they* know, and so on and so on) that your home is for sale. Although the MLS will help you reach prospective buyers who have agents and are actively looking, the market for "just-about-ready-for-prime-time" home buyers is far bigger. Rather than buying a home and living in it for twenty or thirty years, as our parents and grand-parents did, a third of all homeowners seem ready to move if the right opportunity comes along.

Your property might be just what they're waiting for.

A GOOD START

If you want to save money, spread the word that you're about to list your home for sale before you've signed a listing agreement and after you've cleaned and polished your home.

Contact your neighbors (either by leaning over the fence, dropping a flyer in their mailboxes, sending them an e-mail, or leaving a voice-mail message), and let them know you're selling your home and for how much. Your flyer should mimic a listing sheet and contain a photo of the front of your home along with details about its size (including the number of rooms, bedrooms, and bathrooms), amenities, and taxes. Add your name and phone number at the top. At the bottom of the flyer, write, "Please distribute to anyone who might be interested in living in this neighborhood."

Next, spread the word at work that you're selling. Do the same thing at your spouse's or partner's place of employment. Unless you feel uncomfortable with everyone at work knowing how much you think your home is worth, pass out flyers there, too. If your home is close to your office, the short commute may attract prospective buyers. Be sure to talk to family members about your impending sale. A distant cousin might know someone who wants to move into your neighborhood.

Another possibility is to talk about your sale at your children's school. If the school has a bulletin board on which parents can post notices, you should consider posting a few of the details about your home, including the address and your phone number. (You don't necessarily need to include the price, unless you're comfortable doing so.) Parents who know other people who want their children enrolled in your school district can be a great way to find an interested buyer. (It's another reason why you want to buy in a great school district—even if you don't have children.)

Finally, if you live in a condo, a co-op, or a town house, you may have a central meeting place with an area where you can post notices of furniture for sale, baby-sitters wanted, or even units for sale. Sometimes this board exists in the common areas, such as a garage, a laundry room, or a party room. If you have such a place, it's the perfect spot to post a "for sale" notice.

If you do all this marketing before you've listed your home, you're essentially doing a FSBO, but in a targeted way. If someone comes to see your home, it will probably be someone who knows a neighbor, a friend, a relative, or someone at work. Or it's someone whose kids attend your kids' school. If you wait to do this marketing until after your home is listed, you're simply using all your talents and skills to assist your agent in getting your home sold. (Not a bad thing, by the way.)

Listing Agreement Exclusions

If you do this marketing push before your home is listed, and someone comes to see your home, if you don't conclude a deal before you list your home, you might be able to "exclude" that individual on the listing agreement.

When you add someone as an "exclusion" to a listing agreement, what you're doing is saying that if this individual comes back and buys the home, you do not have to pay a commission to the agent. In some cases, you may have to pay some or all of the broker's marketing expenses. While agents will typically allow you to have a couple of exclusions, you won't be able to exclude everyone who has ever seen your home. Think of it as a calculated bet—just in case someone who likes the home and has previously seen it comes back with a decent offer.

You must add your exclusions to the listing agreement before you sign it. Your agent will typically not permit you to alter your exclusions list once the listing is signed.

MAKE YOUR HOME AVAILABLE FOR SHOWINGS

Ten-second drive-by showings are fine and dandy. But if the interior of your house is unavailable for showings, it's unlikely anyone will make an offer on your property.

Being available for showings often means getting your house in order at a moment's notice. That's stressful for most people, and particularly tough for families with young children.

Sally normally keeps an impeccably clean house. But when she and her husband, Tom, were selling their home, making sure the house was ready for a showing at a moment's notice added a huge level of stress to their lives. But knowing that Sally and Tom were always available for showings gave their agent the ability to say yes to any and all requests to see the property. After a few showings, the agent felt very comfortable that Sally and Tom's house would be in immaculate condition no matter what time the showing occurred. The agent felt that the sellers' flexibility and preparedness were instrumental to selling their house quickly and for an excellent price.

There's a big difference between being a homeowner who lists his or her property and being a home seller. A homeowner who lists his property may not be truly committed to getting the deal done unless he's offered the right amount of money. A home seller is someone who has emotionally committed to leaving the property. It almost goes without saying: Selling is a lot easier for the home seller than for a homeowner.

If you want to sell your home as fast and for as much money as possible, say yes to every showing and open-house request. If people can't see your home, it's quite unlikely they'll make an offer to buy it.

A GOOD START

Before you even sign your listing agreement, let your agent know when your home will be available for showings. Make sure the agent understands what times are off-limits. For example, if you have young children who go to sleep early, you might cut off showings at 5 P.M. on weekdays or stretch it to 6 P.M. on a weekend or for a particularly promising prospective buyer who is coming back for a second or third showing. If you and your husband work late and tend to get a slower start in the morning, you might establish a rule that the agent can show the house no earlier than 9 A.M. If that's the case, give the agent additional flexibility in the afternoon and early evenings so she can schedule showings until perhaps 8 P.M. On the weekends, be prepared to show your home all day, even if it means being out of your house from 9 A.M. to 6 P.M. on Saturdays and Sundays.

But no matter what the agreed-to "regular" hours for showings, never turn down a special request. If you live in the city, and have a "city view" of skyscrapers, a buyer may want to have a second or third showing during the evening, when she can be dazzled by the glittering lights. Since the view is a great part of what's being offered for sale, and because most people work during the day and find it hard to leave the office for several hours at a time, you need to be flexible in order to show off your home to its maximum potential.

If you're planning to be out of town, and you are worried about your agent having unfettered access while you're gone, discuss the situation and try to work out a compromise. Perhaps the agent will show the home only during certain hours. Or perhaps, if a lockbox is normally used, the agent will instead agree to meet the buyer and the buyer's agent at the property for every showing while you're out of town to make sure nothing gets disturbed or stolen.

When Ray was selling his home, it was difficult for the agent to get him and his wife to agree to showings. That, plus Ray's insistence that his house was worth about 50 percent more than it finally sold for, delayed the eventual sale of his home for more than six months. Once Ray lowered his price and opened his door, his home sold relatively quickly.

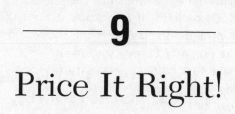

9

Price It Right!

ASSESS THE MARKET BEFORE YOU
PRICE YOUR HOME

If you make a mistake evaluating exactly how fast homes are selling, it can be costly. Home buyers have become quite savvy in
recent years and are very sensitive to list prices. If they feel that
a home is priced even $10,000 higher than it should be, they
could very well decide to ignore the home.

To a seller, this makes no sense at all. You might think, "Well,
why not put in a lower offer, anyway? Just offer what you think
the house is worth."

But it doesn't work that way. As we talked about earlier in the
book, everything you do during the process of selling your home
sends a subliminal message to buyers. The condition of your
home, the price you list at, how you counter an offer—each of
these things will elicit a different reaction from a buyer. And it
can dramatically affect the money you receive at the closing.

For example, while I was writing this book, a house was listed
for sale in my neighborhood. The house is attractive with a large
side yard and a fairly sizable backyard, but it's on a corner lot.
Corner lots can scare people, especially if the house sits close to
the street or to a relatively busy intersection. People might think
the house will be noisy or perhaps dangerous for little kids. All
they can imagine is the noise, and that they'll have to put up a
fence to have a little privacy. So, as buyers are mulling over the
idea, they're mentally adding the cost of an attractive fence to the
price of the property.

If they actually get inside this particular home, they'll discover it's on the small side compared to homes in the neighborhood, and it hasn't been recently renovated. That's another negative, because in addition to the cost of a fence, the home needs to be renovated.

An agent I know who has toured this property with clients says it's priced about 10 percent more than it should be. But the price is apparently a psychological barrier, given all of the perceived negatives of the property. Six months, or even a year ago, this home might have been snapped up by a developer looking for a larger lot—or a buyer willing to pay a premium simply to be in the school district.

The point is that things change—and in real estate, markets can change on a dime. What's hot one week could be slow for the next couple of weeks, before interest picks back up. If this neighbor had priced his property a little lower, he might have generated interest from several different parties, and could well have ended up choosing from a number of different offers. Demand might have pushed up the price of the home nearly to where it is now.

A GOOD START

I'm not necessarily advocating that you underprice or market-price your home, although I think pricing it exactly where the market is should be your goal. What I want you to do is spend time gauging the strength of the market. Think about the following:

- **How many buyers are out there?** While new buyers come in and out of a market every day, try to analyze how strong the demand is for properties in your neighborhood that are similar to yours in price and amenities. Try to visit open houses just before they end (so if a house is open on Sunday from one to four, you should arrive at ten minutes to four), and be sure to glance at the sign-in sheet to count the number of visitors. The number of visitors will change from house to house, and it will depend on the timing (holiday weekends might be slower), the time of year, the weather, and what else is going on in the neighborhood. But it's a good gauge of who is out there. (You may see the same names from house to house, week after week.) Compare the number of names at these open houses to your open-house sign-in sheets to determine if you're getting a similar number of people coming through your property. If you're getting fewer lookers, you have to figure out why (is it the price or the condition of your home?) and what you can do to correct the situation.

- **How many sellers are out there?** Are you competing with 15 houses or 150? Knowing how many other homes are competing for the same buyer will help you to know how aggressive you need to be with pricing. Drive around looking for "for sale" and "for sale by owner" signs. If you live in an area replete with new construction developments, you must count those as competition, as well. Although new homes tend to be pricier than existing ones, remember that if the price differential isn't too much, today's home buyers prefer something new to something older.

- **How fast are houses selling in your area?** Your agent can tell you how quickly homes are selling in your marketplace. Local MLSs should be able to provide detailed data about the average number of days a house sits on the market and the average number of days it takes to close on the sale. If homes are closing in forty-five days, it's a very hot market. If it's taking six months to sell the average home, you're living in a strong buyer's market, which seems to sellers to move at a glacial pace. Also, if you're selling a condo in a neighborhood full of single-family homes, it's going to take longer to move your unit, and the average-time-on-the-market statistics won't provide much guidance. Ask your agent (if she can do so with the MLS data) to isolate how long it's taking homes like yours (condos, co-ops, town houses, or single-family homes) to sell. Unfortunately, there's no way to get your hands on MLS data unless you're working with a Realtor who belongs to the local MLS. So if you're selling by owner or working with a discount brokerage firm on a flat-fee basis, you may not be able to access these numbers.

- **Which homes are selling quickly?** Agents are usually quick to place "under contract" signs on a property. It makes them look like smart, capable agents. But if you're watching closely, you should be able to put your finger on why a particular house went under contract. Look at the amenities each home for sale offers (including size, condition, and special things like a fireplace, a big backyard, or a pool) and look at the home's liabilities (including items that need work, lack of a fireplace, a small yard, and the like). If two homes are almost identical—yes, I know I said there are no identical homes, but let's assume—and they're both listed at the same price, the home that's going to sell first is the one that's perceived by the buying public to be the better value. So if the homes are both the same but one has a new carpet, a buyer will purchase the home with the new carpet first. If one home has a new carpet and the other has a built-in pool, the house with the pool will sell first because it's more expensive to put in an in-ground pool than recarpet a house, so it's perceived as being the better value.

How does your home compare to others that are similar in size and amenities and priced the same (or nearly the same) as yours? If an objective buyer's perception is that another house is a better value than yours, then that house will sell faster than yours will. Your house will not sell until it is perceived by buyers to be the best value in the neighborhood. You can correct this problem by either changing the condition of your home, adding to the amenities, or fixing the liabilities.

Sometimes a house doesn't sell even if it is—in your mind—a better value than all the other homes for sale in a neighborhood. That's because buyers see things differently than sellers, and what you think is a small issue might be a big headache to a buyer. Selling a home is more an art than a science. There is no one right answer. Two nearly identical homes can generate a different selling experience for the owner simply because such details as where on the block the house is located matter.

Over the past dozen years or so, I've talked with thousands of top agents and sellers all over the country, and they all say the same thing: A house priced right for the local market, in the best condition, will generate plenty of interest from prospective buyers. You should have more showings than you know what to do with from the first day you list your property, and receive an offer shortly thereafter. If you gauge the market correctly, put your home in immaculate condition, and price it aggressively, top agents say you should have a good offer in three to four weeks—or less.

Sellers who have followed the steps in this book confirm this is true. Ellyn followed every step I've discussed and received the highest offer anyone in her condo complex had received shortly after listing her apartment by owner. After spending about $5,000 on upgrading the condition of their town house, Phyllis and Ian put up a "for sale" sign in their front yard on a Thursday and had received three offers by the time they held their first open house three days later. The offer they accepted was from the daughter of the homeowner who lived across the street. The buyer was traveling when Phyllis and Ian put their house on the market, and her sister and father put in the winning offer for her. She didn't even see the town house until after her offer had been accepted.

SIMPLE STEP
43

PRICE YOUR HOME ACCURATELY TO REFLECT ITS CONDITION

Nearly everyone I know has little things they live with that may originally have bothered them, but no longer do. Some of these include:

- Dangling lightbulbs—"We haven't found the right fixture yet."

- Dangling wires—"We're waiting for cable/DSL/lighting/fill-in-the-blank to be installed."

- Squeaky doors—"I can't hear a thing!"

- Squeaky floors—"I still can't hear a thing!"

- Fireplace flue that has never been cleaned—"I didn't know that had to be done."

- Dirty air filters in the furnace or air blowers—"I thought those lasted for ten years."

- Broken humidifier—"We never needed it. The house has a lot of natural humidity, particularly in the summer."

- Broken or nonworking water softeners—"Hard water is good for your complexion."

- Broken windows—"That's really just a small, inexpensive fix. Want to see the quote we got?"

- Windows painted shut—"We never use our windows, and sealing them adds to our home's energy efficiency."

- Extension cords all over the place—"We never got around to expanding our electrical service, but don't worry, it's not a fire hazard."

- Broken doorstops—"We haven't found ones strong enough to withstand the constant banging of our children."

- Sticky cabinet doors—"They just need a little household oil."

- Messy landscaping—"I haven't had time to edge the walkway this season."

And the list goes on and on. But when you sell your home, these details are the ones that derail an offer. A prospective buyer will walk around your house looking for reasons *not* to buy your house. Any one of the items I've just listed, or a thousand others, can turn off a buyer to your house—for good. These "liabilities" are items the buyer thinks he has to fix in the first couple of years he lives in your home, including an aging hot-water heater or furnace, old appliances, a leaky roof, broken windows or screens, missing light fixtures, mediocre landscaping, and so on.

A prospective buyer will subtract the actual cost of putting your home into impeccable shape and will probably tack on something extra for the mental pain and anguish it will take to get the job done. They do it logically, because they know the costs, or intuitively thinking, "This house seems older and more run-down, and it'll probably need $20,000 to $30,000 to put it into shape."

And that's how you end up with less money for your house. After all, why haven't you done these things yourself? Because sometimes they're a pain in the neck and you'd rather be doing anything else. The same is true for anyone who will buy your home.

If you've been reading this book from start to finish, you know you should have already polished your home and made it shine. But let's say you either don't have the time, skill, energy, or cash to follow some of these suggestions. You do have an alternative: Leave your home in the condition it's in currently. You can price your home to accurately reflect its condition, or price your home where you want it to be, but accept a lower price that reflects its true condition.

I generally don't encourage selling a home in as-is condition except in certain circumstances.

If you need to make drastic and expensive changes to your home to compete with other homes in your area, then you may be much better off selling it as is. You may not be able to afford the cost of bringing your home up to the neighborhood standard, and you may not have the time or the patience it takes to complete a major overhaul. If this is the case, you may be better off leaving it to the next person who will live in your home.

You're also better off leaving your home in as-is condition if it's destined to be a teardown; that is, if the next owner is simply going to level the house. Perhaps a new house will be built there, or if the house is bought and torn down by one of your neighbors, perhaps he will simply add on to his backyard.

That's what's happening to Beth and Mark's one hundred-year-old house. Their old blue-and-white house is charming, but the land has become so scarce and valuable in their neighborhood, and buyers want fancy amenities and space that their house doesn't have. They could have renovated it, but they decided that with three young children they couldn't stomach moving out while a major renovation was completed. So they ended up selling their land to their two neighbors, both of whom live in brand-new houses that replaced the older homes previously occupying their lots. The two neighbors will split the cost of the land, and Beth and Mark will move to a larger old house that has been renovated nine houses west of where they once lived.

How do you know you're living in a teardown? If the land is now worth more than the house itself, you're living in a teardown. If that's the case, you shouldn't spend another dime on improving your property, but instead look for a developer who does work in the neighborhood and who is looking for an available lot. Once you know what lots are selling for, you should go to your neighbors to see if any of them want a once-in-a-lifetime opportunity to purchase your land to expand their yards. (Perhaps several will purchase your lot and split it.) If adding your land onto their properties will increase the value of their land by more than the cost of purchase, which is probably the case in a hot neighborhood of teardowns, then you'll likely be able to sell to them, without incurring a commission.

Leslie had lived in her home for more than twenty-five years, and raised her daughter there by herself after her divorce. But her house was tiny (less than 1,500 square feet), one story, cramped, and packed with stuff. With all the development in the area, her house had outlived its usefulness. The entire value of the property was in the land. So Leslie began marketing her home to developers. She sold it for nearly $300,000. The developer tore down the house and put up a brand-new, 3,000-square-foot house, which was then sold for $1 million.

If you're dead set against having your home torn down, another option is to wait until someone comes along who falls in love with your house and your land and is willing to tackle the headaches and cost of a major renovation. While there aren't too many fixer-upper families out there, someone will always be looking for a bargain. To attract that person's attention, you'll have to price your property correctly.

But if you are dead set against having your house torn down, you have to understand one thing: You still have the mind-set of a homeowner, not a home seller.

A GOOD START

In a hot neighborhood, developers (or their agents) will often either knock on doors or send letters to residents asking if they plan on selling anytime soon. The developers are hoping to get their offer in front of the seller first, but they are also hoping to buy a home for a little less if they get it before it goes on the market.

If this happens to you, make sure you know how much your home is worth before you sign the contract to sell your home. Contact an agent or two in the neighborhood and ask how much teardown homes are being sold for. If you don't know exactly how much your property is worth as a teardown, you could easily underprice your home by tens or hundreds of thousands of dollars. That's profit you've automatically transferred to the developer's pocket.

If your home is a potential fixer-upper, instead of a teardown, you'll probably get more for it, but not as much as finished homes in the neighborhood are fetching. For example, I was recently in a house that needs to have the kitchen gutted. While the space was workable, there is a screened-in porch just off the kitchen. If the porch space was winterized and incorporated into a huge fabulous kitchen with skylights, it could seriously raise the value of the home. How much? Let's say doing the work (with granite countertops, stainless-steel appliances, and a hardwood floor, plus some structural work to incorporate the back-porch space) would cost $65,000. It could easily raise the value of the home by $100,000, a gain of $35,000.

So if you were selling this house in as-is condition, you might subtract $65,000 to $90,000 off the price of a totally done home in the area. If a home is worth $500,000, you'd sell yours for perhaps $425,000. By knowing what a done home is worth in your neighborhood, and how much it would cost to fix whatever problem you have, you have a starting point for working up a list price that will make sense to a prospective buyer.

An Agent Can Help

Pricing your home to accurately reflect its condition is difficult, and that's why you probably should hire an experienced agent who can help you price your home right from the start.

Talk to the agent about homes that are done in the neighborhood and how they're priced. Then talk to the agent about what it would take to get your home into that condition (if it's at all possible). Next, try to estimate how much it would cost to put your home into that shape.

Talk to a contractor or two about how much it might cost to complete the work. If the changes are structural (like moving walls, plumbing, and appliances or fixtures), then tack on an extra 10 to 20 percent for things like an architect's fee and hidden problems. Having a good idea of the costs and timing involved to complete the work will help you more accurately price your home to reflect its condition.

Of course, the big benefit of pricing your home right for its physical condition and local market conditions is that you'll sell it faster and for more money because you'll generate the maximum amount of interest from potential buyers.

IF THERE'S NO RESPONSE, LOWER YOUR PRICE

Sellers don't want to lower the price of their homes. And when you're selling, you won't want to lower your list price, either. A lower list price means more cash coming right off the top, and that's profit out of your pockets. Or you may feel you *need* to get a certain amount of money out of your home, so you can't lower the price.

If you've followed the advice in this book, you likely won't find yourself in this situation. But sometimes circumstances change or you'll make a mistake and your home will suddenly be overpriced for the local market.

How do you know if your home is overpriced? If you don't get an immediate response from agents wanting to set up showings, it's a bad sign. If you don't have one or two very serious buyers within a couple of weeks, people who have been back a few times to see what you have, it's a bad sign. And if you don't have a valid offer within four to six weeks, you may be in trouble.

(The exception to the rule—and there always is one—is for high-end sellers. If you're selling a home for a price that's near the top of the market in your area, it could take longer to sell simply because there aren't that many wealthy people looking to buy homes. Talk to your agent—who should be very experienced at this—about how long he or she thinks it will take to sell a high-end home in your area. She might say six months to a year. Or she might say the market is strong right now, so ninety days.)

If you've hardly had any showings, and no offers, six weeks after listing your home, you can either pull your home off the market or you can lower your purchase price. The question is, by how much?

A GOOD START

You have to know how much over the market price you are before you can start lowering the list price of your home. Remember, the goal is to meet the market.

One way to gauge this is to do some additional market research. That means going out and looking at homes similar to yours that have recently sold or have been listed. Ask your agent to provide you with the addresses and sales prices for all homes similar to yours in your area ("comps") that have recently sold. You won't be able to get the selling price for properties that have gone under contract, but your agent may know approximately what the contract price is or can give you an educated guess. Try to find a relationship between the size and amenities of these homes and the price at which an offer has been made.

You might also ask your agent what price she thinks your home should be listed at given current market conditions. Undoubtedly, your agent will have an opinion on the subject—if she doesn't, you may have a larger problem than a mispriced home.

I generally think that a price drop will get the most notice if it's significant. Depending on the price of the home, and where the market is, if you drop the price by $500, no one will care. If you drop the price by 2 to 5 percent, that's going to get noticed in a big way. So if your home is priced at $200,000, and you drop it to $194,500, you should get a reaction. If you price it at $193,500, you'll get more of a reaction. The pricier the home, the more dramatic-looking your drop will be, but the percentage ought to stay the same.

When should you be more aggressive with a price drop? If your home has a serious defect (such as location), and it hasn't sold, you may have to drop the price more dramatically. (Location defects could include a railroad running at the back of your property, being located on the corner of a busy intersection, or living near an industrial plant.) If you drop the price 2 or 3 percent and still don't have much interest in your home within two to four weeks, you should consider yet another price drop of 2 to 3 percent.

Finally, don't worry about underpricing your home. Homes that underprice the market tend to generate multiple offers, which raises the ultimate selling price of the property.

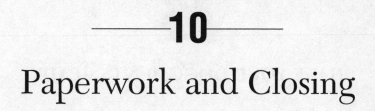

10
Paperwork and Closing

HAVE YOUR DOCUMENTS READY

Whether you're buying or selling a home, you'll be buried in paperwork. (Remember the thousands of times you signed your name when you bought your house?) While selling is less cumbersome, there is a mass of papers you'll want to organize and have on hand, just waiting for a prospective buyer to ask for them.

Here is a list of important documents or paperwork you'll want to be able to lay your hands on at a moment's notice:

- **Closing book.** When you bought your home, your attorney or title or escrow agent should have handed you a folder with all the paperwork from the transaction. This might have included a copy of your offer to purchase, the signed contract, a copy of the title insurance policy, your HUD-1 sheet (detailing all your closing costs and those of the buyer), your loan documents, and so forth. Although it's unlikely you'll need these documents, you never know. It's best to keep them handy, just in case.

- **Mortgage, home equity loan, or refinance documents.** If you have a home loan or have taken out a home equity loan, you should have copies of those loan documents handy. If you can't find your loan documents, you'll need the loan number (or numbers) and the loan servicer's toll-free customer-service number.

- **Home warranty.** A home warranty is an extended service warranty for an older home. It guarantees to a buyer that all the mechanical systems (like air-conditioning) and appliances (like your refrigerator) that are working in the house the day of closing will work for a year. If something breaks, the buyer can call a toll-free number, pay a service fee (of anywhere from $50 to $150 or higher), and someone will come and either fix the item or replace it. If you plan to purchase a home warranty for your home, or have already done so (many home warranty programs cover the seller while he or she is actively selling the property, in addition to covering the buyer for the first year he or she lives in the home), you'll want to have that paperwork handy. Many buyers know they should ask for a home warranty, but are confused as to what is really covered by the policy. Having it handy could help straighten out any confusion. (See "A Good Start" in Step 1 for more information about home warranties.)

- **Proof of problems resolved.** If you've had a problem with water, like a leak in the basement, but you've since fixed it, you'll want to keep proof of the repair close at hand. So keep all the bills and receipts for payment from contractors or workmen you've employed through the years. Buyers may want to see proof of a repair to be sure that you have taken care of a problem. If the repair carried a warranty that will transfer to the new owner, be sure to include any warranty provided. For example, if you've waterproofed the basement, and the repair carried a five-year warranty and there are four years left on the warranty, you will want to be able to pass along the warranty information to the new buyer of your home.

- **Warranties on appliances, mechanical systems, and the like.** If you have bought a new refrigerator, dishwasher, or washer and dryer, the manufacturers' warranties should be kept together in a warranty file for your new buyer. He or she will appreciate being able to look at all the home's warranties, whether or not they've expired, in one place.

- **Renovation information.** In addition to keeping proof of your repair work on hand, you should collect all the information from a recent expansion or renovation for your prospective buyer. Collect warranty information, bills, and receipts, and keep them in a file that you can easily access in case questions come up. You'll also want to have your building permits, certificate of occupancy, plans, surveys, and a list of contractors and subcontractors who worked on your home. If you had plans drawn up for a potential renovation that you decided not to do, it's a kindness to include the plans in this renovation kit for your future home buyers. It will give them a good start if they decide to do some work to the house in the future.

- **Condominium or co-op documents.** If you live in a condo or co-op, future buyers will want to see copies of the building budget for the last two years, plus minutes from the prior year or two of board meetings. Buyers may also ask for a copy of the "condo dec.," which is the legal condo declaration that was written and filed when the condo was created. You should also have copies of the homeowner's association (whether it is a condo or co-op or town house) rules, regulations, and bylaws for buyers to look at. If your building or association has specific rules about pets, especially if dogs or cats are not allowed, you're doing yourself a favor by letting prospective buyers know this up front. The one thing that can kill a deal down the line is finding out that Tabby won't be permitted to move in with the buyer after closing. In fact, one agent lost three apartments for her buyers when each building disclosed well after the offer had been accepted that building rules limited the number of pets to one or two animals; these buyers had three cats, which excluded them from nearly every building.

- **Bills, the cost of basic living expenses, and other paperwork.** Buyers will want to know the cost of heating and cooling your home during the past year, how much you typically pay for your gas bill each month, and the amount of your property taxes. If you live in a two- or three-family (known as a two-flat or three-flat, or multifamily building in other parts of the country) building, or rent out the attic or basement of your property, the new buyers will want to see copies of the signed leases. Make sure you keep this paperwork together in one file so that it's easy for the buyer to look at all of the relevant information about your home.

- **Listing sheets.** Keep a few dozen extra listing sheets on hand, just in case someone wants an extra. You never know when and where you'll want to hand these out.

A GOOD START

Gather your house-related documents and make photocopies of them. You'll need more listing sheets than anything else, so make plenty of copies of those. If you live in a condo or a co-op, have a few sets of the condo or co-op documents on hand, so serious buyers can look them over for any problems (like the pet exclusion) and perhaps take home a copy for future reference.

The documents that are for you and your attorney can easily be kept in a file folder either with or near your other important papers. If you can't find any of these documents, call your real-estate attorney to see if he or she kept the originals or copies of them.

SIMPLE STEP
46

HIRE A REAL-ESTATE ATTORNEY

Your personal real-estate attorney (not the one hired by the mortgage company that you pay for) is the only person in the deal whose fee doesn't depend on you closing on the sale (or purchase, for that matter) of your property. His or her entire job is to protect you, and only you, during your sale.

Everyone else has an interest in making sure you close the transaction so that they can get paid. Neither the buyer's agent nor your agent gets paid unless the deal closes. The lenders don't get paid (or paid off) until the deal closes. And, the closing agent doesn't get paid until you close.

Whether you use an attorney to help you sell your home is often a matter of local custom. No state will require you to use one, though if you don't use one in Chicago, New York, or Boston, it's as if you've just hung a sign on your back that says "kick me." On the other hand, people will look at you strangely in California, Georgia, or parts of Indiana if you say you want to use an attorney, because in those states and several others, closing agents handle the paperwork for the closings and you, the seller, are left to read and sign documents on your own. The closing agent doesn't represent you or the buyer. You have no representative at the closing to watch out for your best interests. In a state where attorneys draft and negotiate the closing documents, the attorney is your advocate.

When should you hire an attorney?

- **If you are selling by owner.** If you have been lucky enough to sell without an agent, you'll need someone to prepare the documents, help arrange the details of the closing, tell you what disclosures the law requires you to make to your buyer, and deal with any sorts of problems or issues that come up during the title search or inspection.

- **If you live in a state where attorneys are commonly used.** In states where attorneys are used to close deals, you will find that not having one is a hindrance. Why? You will have to obtain all the documents needed for the closing, as well as draft them without an attorney advising you who is knowledgeable about real estate and your state's laws. It will be up to you to check out the title to the property and purchase title insurance. If you need to provide certain disclosures to the buyer, and you're not working with an agent, you will have to contact the state's real-estate commission to find out which disclosures are mandatory and how you are required by law to make them.

- **If you don't trust your agent.** Sometimes agent-seller relationships that start well end badly. If this is the case, you'll want someone on your side to make sure that the deal goes smoothly. An attorney can help to keep a healthy distance between you and your agent, or the buyer, if there are problems.

- **If your deal is complicated.** If you are selling a small piece of a larger property that you own, or if you have a skittish, nitpicking buyer who wants to make a lot of "little" changes to the contract, or if there are some other complications, you'll want to have legal counsel on hand. The attorney can also help you resolve title issues regarding easements and surveys and answer difficult questions.

- **If the buyer doesn't satisfy the terms of the contract.** When home buyers sign a contract, they often include contingencies which allow them to back out of the deal. For example, they might have a financing contingency, which permits them to kill the deal if they can't qualify for the size mortgage they need. Or they might have an inspection contingency, which allows them to back out if the house doesn't pass inspection. All these contingencies should have time limits on them. In other words, they expire within, say, ten days. If a buyer can't get his act together to get the inspection done within ten days, he or she loses the right to back out if the inspection is unsatisfactory. The attorney keeps track of these expiration dates and makes sure the buyer lives up to the terms and conditions of the offer or contract for purchase.

Attorneys can help in other ways, as well. They:

- Help remove emotion from the deal by keeping an objective point of view.
- Can negotiate the finer points of the contract for you.
- Can protect you from getting a bad deal if the negotiations turn nasty.
- Can work with the brokers to organize and finalize the details of the closing.
- Can explain the legal consequences of the deal and any terms you may not understand.
- Are a good buy for the money, as you can usually hire a real-estate attorney for a fixed fee for a residential transaction (as long as you stay away from the big firms in town).
- May be able to get you a reduced fee from the title company for certain fees you pay.
- Track all the details of a closing, from working on the closing documents with your lender to figuring out the tax (and other) prorations.

- Draft and prepare all the closing documents.

- Obtain the necessary approvals, certificates, and, in some cases, transfer stamps for the closing.

- Provide you with a closing book that neatly organizes all the documents involved with your house closing.

If I haven't yet made the case for hiring a real-estate attorney, let me just remind you that we live in an increasingly litigious society. Anyone who watches Court TV or any of the "Judge" shows, knows you can sue anyone for any reason (real or made up) and have your day (or many, many days) in court. All it takes is time and money. And when it comes to buying and selling homes, our emotions tend to run high. While lawsuits don't happen every day, frequently things do go wrong at the closing. What an attorney can do is take a difficult situation, where something has gone wrong, and try to smooth it over enough to get the deal done.

A GOOD START

You may think you're saving money by not hiring a real-estate attorney. And, in some cases, you might be. Studies (usually paid for by some national real-estate organization) show that buyers and sellers who don't use attorneys spend $150 to $200 less than buyers and sellers who do use attorneys.

Big deal. Here you are, selling your single largest asset. While there are a lot of fees when you sell your home (with more coming, as many states have recently raised their fees for recording documents and transferring property), why wouldn't you spend an extra $150 to know that someone is out there watching your back?

In most states where real-estate attorneys are commonly used, you pay a flat fee for the attorney's services. The fee might run $350 to $1,000, but often the attorney can get you a break on some of the other fees you'll pay for, like title insurance. Or if the title company you choose pays your attorney to do the title search, you'll probably pay a very nominal fee for closing on your home because the attorney also makes money from the title-insurance company. (I don't recommend doing this, by the way, because if something goes wrong, and the attorney misses something on the title report, you could be out a serious chunk of money if the title-insurance policy doesn't cover the problem. You're much better off buying your title insurance from a national title company. See "A Good Start" in Step 47 for a few suggestions.)

If you compare the cost of using an attorney to the cost of using a closing company in a state that doesn't use attorneys, you will find that the difference between the two is nominal—if anything at all. But even if you live in a state that doesn't use attorneys to close house deals, the extra money you might pay to have an attorney review your documents and help you close the deal could amount to a few hundred dollars. Let's say your home is worth $200,000, and you're going to pay $500 extra to have an attorney review all your documents, help you negotiate, and take care of shepherding your documents around. Sounds like a pretty fair return for the money spent.

I think it's such a good deal, and so important in our litigious society, that you should hire an attorney even in states where attorneys aren't commonly used.

As readers of my other books and listeners to my radio show know, my husband, Sam, is a real-estate attorney. For the past fifteen years or so, I've watched him close thousands of real-estate transactions. Most of the time, deals close smoothly. But sometimes, perhaps one or two deals out of ten, something goes wrong or has been forgotten. It's then that the real-estate attorney proves his or her worth.

Unfortunately, you never know when that's going to happen.

To find a good real-estate attorney, ask your agent for a few names. Ask your friends which attorney they used to close on their home, and if they liked the person they worked with. If no one knows any attorneys, you can call your local or state bar association and ask for a list of attorneys who practice real-estate law in your state. You can also ask your local bar association to put you in touch with the attorney who heads the bar's real-estate law council or division. That individual should know some of the better real-estate attorneys in your area and can provide you with several names. Once you get a few names, you can call and talk to the attorney about how much experience he has had with residential closings, how many he does a year, and what he charges to review documents and handle the closing.

When you hire the attorney, make sure you get a written letter outlining the services that will be provided and the fee that will be charged for those services. The letter is called an "engagement letter," and attorneys are required to give them to you so that you can decide whether to hire them. If your attorney blows off the engagement letter, it's a serious refutation of state law. That's not the kind of individual I'd want to represent me, because this person doesn't respect the laws they've been trained to uphold.

SHOP AROUND TO LOWER YOUR CLOSING COSTS

While many closing costs are fixed for the seller (your state transfer tax, for example, might be $3 for every $500 of sales price), some costs can be shopped around, including your survey and the title-insurance policy.

In some states, sellers choose the title company and pay for the title-insurance policy because it's up to the seller to prove that he or she owns clear title to the property. In other words, you have to prove you own it, and that's why you buy the title insurance. In other states, the buyer selects the title company and pays for the insurance policy.

If you use an attorney, he or she probably has a favorite title company. If you're in a state where attorneys aren't generally used to close deals, or you've elected not to use one, your closing agent probably has a preferred title company he or she likes to use (or is part of the escrow company). Either way, you are *not* obligated to use the title or escrow company that the attorney or agent recommends. You should shop around for the lowest costs for these services. Be aware, however, that many states regulate title-insurance-policy costs and escrow-closing fees. In these states, the state sets the fees, and they are nonnegotiable. (As a side note, sellers who live in states that do not regulate the cost of title insurance pay *far* less for these policies and services than sellers in states that do regulate them.)

Just make sure that you choose solid companies that aren't going to disappear with the funds before you close. And before you say, "Naw, that'll never happen!" let me tell you about Intercounty Title Company, a title company that used to do business in Chicago.

One day, Intercounty Title, which had been in operation for years, just closed its doors. At that time, they were holding millions of dollars in funds for residential and commercial real-estate transactions that had closed or were closing that day. No one knew where the principals were, and no one knew where the money had gone. Checks bounced, lenders were not paid, and sellers didn't receive the proceeds from the sale of their properties.

The better real-estate attorneys hadn't been using Intercounty because of its reputation. But a lot of people got caught. Almost everyone eventually got their money, but it was a mess, and it took time.

Even stranger things than this have happened, and you don't want them to happen to you.

A GOOD START

There's nothing wrong with shopping around to make sure you're getting the best deal on your title insurance or escrow closing. But make sure you really do your homework. Before you agree to use a company or service:

- **Check them out.** Go to the Better Business Bureau site (www.bbb.org) to make sure there are no complaints against the company. If it's a title or escrow company, you should also check with the state agency that licenses and regulates these companies to make sure no one has filed complaints against them. (Typically, you'd contact the state's real-estate commission.) Finally, you can check with the attorney general's office or your state office of consumer protection to make sure no one has filed a grievance or accused the company of fraud or mismanagement of funds.

- **Ask for a list of fees.** Title and escrow companies usually have standard fees that are printed on a card. It's a little like a rate card for a hotel. You simply call and ask for their rate card. The fees listed will always be the most you can pay. In some states, where fees are not regulated, they will be negotiable. (By the way, you'll generally pay *much* less for title insurance if you live in a state where title insurance is *not* regulated by the government. In those states, a competitive marketplace drives prices down.)

- **Ask for a discount.** As with anything else, you may get a discount simply by asking for it, if you live in a state where title and escrow company's fees are not regulated. I once interviewed an executive with one of the leading title companies in the country, and he said that his company offered discounts to sellers who asked for them. So check it out, and press the title-company representative to give you the best deal possible. While an attorney should get you the best rate (simply because he or she brings so much business to the title or escrow company), savvy consumers often do better than the professionals simply by asking nicely.

- **Get it in writing.** It's always a good idea to get the rate quote in writing. That way, you can prove what you were offered, should you need to do so.

On the Web

There are a number of national title companies (that also provide escrow services) that maintain excellent Web sites.

You can use these Web sites to educate yourself about title insurance or escrow services and why you might need them:

Stewart Title, also known as Land America Title: Stewart.com or LandAm.com

Chicago Title & Trust, also known as Fidelity National Financial: CTT.com or FNF.com

Ticor Title: Ticortitle.com

First American Title Insurance Company: FirstAm.com

Commonwealth Land Title Insurance Company: CLTIC.com

Lawyer's Title: LTIC.com

11

When Nothing's Working

GIVE THE BUYER A BREAK

If your home isn't selling, there may be a problem with either its condition or price. But sometimes buyers need an extra nudge. There are things you can do that will effectively lower the net amount you take away from the deal, but could help get your home sold. If you're having trouble selling and haven't received an offer, perhaps these suggestions will help:

- **Pay your buyer's closing costs.** A buyer (particularly if you're selling in the first-time buyer market) may want to purchase your home, but may not be able to afford all the cash costs, including closing costs or the amount the lender will require the buyer to have in reserve (in a savings account, in case something breaks). Instead of turning away a prospective buyer, consider paying some or all of his or her closing costs. While it might cost you an extra one or two thousand, you may be able to keep the price of your home a little higher (because the buyer can finance it) while solving your buyer's cash-flow problem.

- **Buy down the buyer's mortgage.** If the buyer can't easily manage the monthly mortgage payments on your home after purchasing it, you may want to buy down the buyer's mortgage. A buydown loan can lower the monthly payments for a period of three to five years. Here's how it works: You pay the difference between what the buyer would have paid with a market-rate loan in the first few years and an interest rate that is lower. For example, in the first year of a buydown loan, if the going interest rate on a thirty-year mortgage is 7 percent, you might buy down the buyer's loan so it appears to be 6 percent. The second year, the loan carries an interest rate of 6.25 percent (instead of 7 percent). The third year, the loan rate is 6.5 percent. The fourth year, it rises to 6.75 percent. In the final year, it's back to where it should be—7 percent. You pay the difference between where the rate is and where it should be, which may be only a couple of thousand dollars. But it might be enough to get the buyer to purchase your home over another down the street.

- **Offer seller financing.** Seller financing is when you, for whatever reason, opt to act as the lender for a prospective buyer. In the past, buyers liked seller financing because it was cheaper for them and easier than going to a conventional lender. These days, conventional lenders are so flexible and so competitively priced that it's hard to imagine someone who is creditworthy but can't get a mortgage. Seller financing should be a last resort for you, if you do it at all. If you do decide to offer seller financing, you'll want to do it only for someone who has great credit (and who therefore should be able to get a bank loan). To make sure you don't take any unnecessary risks, be sure to hire a real-estate attorney to draft the paperwork and help you qualify the buyer. If your buyer doesn't need a first loan, but a small second mortgage, you could offer that for a short period of time, say two to five years. But the risk is still huge because you'll be second in line behind the main lender. Again, I don't recommend doing seller financing. If you're faced with a situation where the buyer will walk if you don't do seller financing, I'd find another buyer.

- **Offer to solve a specific problem.** Rosemary's three-unit condo building has a problem. The parking spaces that the developer sold with the units really accommodate only two cars, not three. So every night, one of the three unit owners is looking for parking on the street. In Rosemary's neighborhood, parking can be very tight, so a person might be circling for fifteen minutes or more until he or she finds a parking spot. If you have a problem like that, consider offering to pay for a year's worth of parking for the buyer who purchases your home. While it doesn't solve the problem for good, it could be just enough to seal the deal. If your homeowner's association is about to levy a special assessment, offer to pay part or all of the special assessment. (At least you won't have to live through the work.)

- **Offer freebies.** What could make your property more attractive to a buyer? Try a freebie. During the Gulf War and the recession of the early 1990s, many sellers offered buyers (and their brokers) all sorts of extras, including gift certificates to fancy shops and department stores, free trips to Disney World (airfare included), cars (one seller I know offered the buyer a used Mercedes), cash for decorating their new home, meals at fancy restaurants, massages, and all sorts of other stuff. While these things will cost you money, they may draw more attention to your property.

- **Offer to pay a year's worth of real-estate taxes.** This will cost you a chunk of change, but it may give you an edge.

A GOOD START

Talk to your agent about what you can do to increase the odds of selling a tough property. While lowering your price is one way to do it, you may be able to achieve the same result by offering one of the freebies I've suggested and walk away with more money in your pocket.

For example, let's say you have a house that's worth $500,000. If it's overpriced, you could either lower the price

$40,000, or offer a brand-new $20,000 car as a freebie. You'll do better if you can get someone to bite on the new car rather than lowering your price that much, and the idea of buying a house, and getting a new car thrown in, may be just what some buyer out there is looking for.

Remember, the idea behind freebies and special offers is to raise awareness of your home. Buyers like deals, and they may be drawn in by the deal you're offering.

Getting the Word Out

If you're going to offer special terms with the sale of your home, you should let as many people know as possible. Your first step is to ask your agent to include the special terms of the deal in your MLS listing. Your listing sheet should also spell out whatever you're offering, whether it's a car or a free vacation or a $10,000 decorating allowance. But remember that once you commit yourself in writing to that deal, it's out there unless you put a specific time limit on it. For example, you might say "Free car for 30 days" or "Free car until January." If you leave it open-ended, and then drop your price, you could end up with a buyer who is expecting to pay the lower list price *and* get whatever freebie you promised when the list price was higher.

SIMPLE STEP
49

OFFER A BONUS TO THE BROKER
WHO BRINGS THE BUYER

Typically, real-estate commissions get split equally between the buyer's agent and the seller's agent. So if the total commission you pay is 5 percent, each side would get 2.5 percent of the sales price (which is then further split between each agent and the firm he or she works for). If you hire a discount broker, a 4 percent total commission might be split differently, with 2.5 to 3 percent going to the buyer's agent and just 1 percent to the listing agent.

However the fee gets split, you don't want the buyer's agent getting the short end of the stick, or you'll find fewer buyers showing up at your door.

If your house isn't selling, you may want to offer the buyer's agent a bonus if he or she brings the buyer who ultimately closes on the property. How much of a bonus? It could be $500 or $2,500, depending on the sales price of the home. While no self-respecting agent will force his or her buyer to purchase your property just because of the bonus, most agents will make sure any client they have who might be right for your property gets in to see it.

A GOOD START

Make sure your listing agent includes information about the buyer-broker bonus in the MLS. If the buyer's agent doesn't know about the bonus, your incentive will be wasted because it won't generate the kind of traffic you're expecting.

You should also talk over the idea of offering a bonus to the buyer's agent with your own agent. While he or she should understand your frustration at not having sold your home, and your interest in doing anything to attract more buyers, there could be some hurt feelings. Gently remind your agent that offering a bonus to the buyer's agent is just one more tool you feel is necessary to sell your home.

Occasionally, you'll find that your agent will unexpectedly shoot you in the foot. When Sally sold her home in Atlanta, she used a family friend. She was so sure the agent was looking out for her best interest that she never asked what the commission split would be with the buyer's broker. She assumed it would be shared equally; since the total commission was 6 percent, that would be 3 percent for each agent.

Wrong! The family friend decided to split the commission so that she received 3.5 percent and the buyer's agent received only 2.5 percent. When Sally found out, she was extremely upset, but it explained why few buyers were being shown her home. Make sure you ask your listing agent (even if the agent is your mother) what the split is going to be with the buyer's agent *before* you sign your listing agreement.

SIMPLE STEP 50

LISTEN TO THE BUYERS—AND THEIR AGENTS

Who's to blame when a house doesn't sell quickly? If you ask the seller, he or she will often point to the broker.

But if you're going to start pointing fingers, you might as well start with yourself. Regardless of what the broker says and does, it's ultimately your home. And that means it's up to you to stay on top of things, pinpoint where the situation got out of whack, and come up with a solution.

Consider what happened to my neighbors, an elderly couple who have lived in their house for nearly fifty years. They decided they wanted something a little newer and definitely on one floor, so that the husband, who uses a walker, could get around more easily.

They hired a broker they knew, who immediately handed off the listing to a new associate. For four long months, only two people came to see the house. The broker never held an open house or a broker's open. She rarely advertised the house for sale in the newspaper.

At the end of the four months, the couple terminated the listing agreement and hired a different brokerage firm. While they liked the firm's managing broker, they weren't crazy about the agent who actually listed the property. After two weeks, they asked for a meeting to change agents, but the managing broker advised them to stick it out. The agent held a few open houses, advertised the house, and made a lot of phone calls. Still, no one made an offer. At the end of the ninety-day listing, the couple fired the firm, and decided to wait until spring to try to sell again. If you're wondering, "What's wrong with this picture?" you've asked the right question. While the first broker just let the house sit there, she helped the owners set the original list price for the property. While the house is large, it is old and in need of some care. In particular, the slate roof has a large spot of green moss growing on it, which is visible from the street. Though it wouldn't cost much to have it removed, the owners have chosen not to do it, though they can show a prospective buyer several letters from roofers who attest to the excellent physical condition of the roof.

Still, you have to assume that prospective buyers were driving by the property, looking at the green stuff growing on the roof, and driving on. The house, which was priced correctly, didn't sell because the sellers failed to do their job of getting the house into the kind of shape that would meet a prospective buyer's expectations.

Buyers and their agents can be a tremendous source of information about your home. And, if probed correctly, they can easily identify what derailed an offer. It might be the price or the location, or it might be something that's wrong with the house itself, or it might be that they simply don't like your decorating. Whatever the reason, this kind of feedback is invaluable.

If you're getting a large number of prospective buyers coming through your doors, but no one is making an offer, you should try to find out why. Fixing this problem (if you can—and if you can't, then fixing it by lowering the price) should bring in an offer.

A GOOD START

If you have a fair number of buyers coming through your property without making an offer, ask your agent to start calling back the buyers' agents to find out what's holding everyone back. Your agent has to tread carefully here, because he or she doesn't want the buyers' agents to disclose confidential information.

Once you find out what's wrong with your property (and after you get over any hurt feelings you may have because someone doesn't like your home), it's up to you to fix whatever is wrong.

Why? Because ultimately, and despite all the money you'll shell out for the agent's commission, the listing agent can't sell your home. Your home has to sell itself. The only way that's going to happen is if you face up to whatever problems or issues exist and solve them.

TOP TEN MISTAKES
A HOME SELLER MAKES

Selling a home is tough, even under the best of circumstances. But when you fall into one of these ten traps, it can be impossible. Here are the top ten mistakes home sellers make, with my hope that if you know what's ahead, you can avoid these pitfalls.

1. Not knowing why you're selling. Are you selling because you want to or because you have to? Knowing the answer to that question will fundamentally color your selling experience. If you're selling because you want to, you can afford to take a more laid-back approach, price your home higher, and choose a less aggressive agent. If you're selling because you have to, your desperation will reveal itself in your list price and the type of agent you hire.

2. Not preparing your home for sale. You can sell in as-is condition, but you won't get as much money for your home, and you won't sell it as quickly as you will if you spruce it up and keep it clean. Today's buyers want a home that requires as little work as possible—preferably just moving in their furniture and hanging their art.

3. Choosing the wrong broker, or no broker. If you don't choose the right broker, you can have a perfectly awful selling experience. But choosing to go it alone may not be the right answer, either. People who sell by owner (FSBOs) and allow their homes to linger on the market for months or years aren't doing themselves any favors—and they're not saving money, either.

4. Overpricing your home. When you sell a home, everything is about price, condition, and the current state of the marketplace. If you're not priced right for the actual condition of your home, or type of market you're in, you could wait a long time for a good offer.

5. Hanging around during showings. Unless you're doing an FSBO, selling by owner without an agent, you have no business hanging around the property while your agent shows it. Frankly, if you're a prospective buyer, it's creepy to have a seller present during a showing, looking over your shoulder while you're trying to decide whether there's enough closet space for your stuff. So if you want to sell, stay away during showings. And if you are doing an FSBO, and have to be there to show the property, don't say too much.

6. Owning a smelly house. Pet smells and other odors cling to the carpets, drapes, furniture, and other soft surfaces. Cigarette or cigar smoke can even permeate into wallpaper and paint. If your house smells of anything unpleasant, be it pets, smoke, strong food odors, or even babies' diapers, it'll be a tough sell.

7. Letting your house or broker go stale. If a house sits on the market too long, it can seem stale. That is, buyers and other agents will start to wonder what's wrong, which can lead to fewer showings and no offers. If your house has been on the market for three months without an offer, you have a problem. At the end of six months without an offer, you should either pull your home off the market for a while and retool, change agents, or dramatically lower your price.

8. Failing to recognize a good offer. Agents like to say that the first offer is the best offer. But sellers, thinking that something better may be just around the corner, often take a pass on the first offer, only to regret it down the line. If you get an offer, and it is close to or above your minimum sales price, you should treat it as *the* offer and try to make the deal work out.

9. Not making your final mortgage payment before closing. Some sellers don't realize that they must still make every mortgage payment on time, even if they have signed a contract to sell their home. Even if they're closing on the second day of the month. When the escrow officer or attorney draws up the closing documents, the numbers are calculated based on the payments that have been (or should have been) received by the lender. Since your monthly payment is probably due on the first of the month, you need to make that final mortgage payment, even if you're closing the next day, or all the calculations will be off, and you could be hit with a late fee or penalties, plus a ding on your credit history.

10. Setting the wrong closing date for tax purposes. Uncle Sam has given all sellers a great gift—as long as you lived in your home for two of the past five years, you can take the first $250,000 (up to $500,000 if you're married) in profits tax-free. What some sellers don't understand is that they can't live in a home for eighteen months and take three-quarters of the maximum profit tax-free. Unless you're moving fifty miles away to take a new job or have to sell for a specific health reason, it doesn't work that way. If you close on your home having lived there only twenty-three months (instead of twenty-four), you'll owe long-term capital gains tax on any profit you have made on your home. And for some sellers, that's a substantial amount (and a costly penalty). So be sure to stay in your home for at least twenty-four months before you sell.

APPENDIX

2

ROOM-BY-ROOM CHECKLIST

Use this checklist to make sure your home is in perfect shape before each showing.

Living Room

_____ Furniture straightened, cushions plumped and smoothed

_____ Surfaces empty and dusted, carpet vacuumed, floors washed or swept

_____ Bookshelves neat and organized, papers put away

_____ Focal point of room clearly visible and in order

Dining Room

_____ Table dusted, chairs straight, table clear or set with nice place mats

_____ Floor dusted, carpet vacuumed

_____ Art straightened, silver polished and attractively dislayed

_____ Focal point of room clearly visible and in order

Family Room

_____ Furniture straightened, cushions plumped and smoothed

_____ Surfaces empty and dusted, carpet vacuumed, floors washed or swept

_____ Bookshelves neat and organized, papers put away

_____ Children's toys organized; videos, tapes, and CDs put
away

_____ Focal point of room clearly visible and in order

Office

_____ Furniture straightened, cushions plumped and smoothed

_____ Surfaces empty and dusted, carpet vacuumed, floors
washed or swept

_____ Bookshelves neat and organized, papers put away

_____ Private papers stored, computer and printer turned off, fax
machine unplugged

_____ Closet organized, file cabinets locked

_____ Focal point of room clearly visible and in order

Kitchen

_____ Countertops empty (except for a few attractive items) and
cleaned, floor washed or swept, cabinets organized (don't
forget under the sink), garbage thrown away (no smells),
vase of fresh flowers

_____ Bookshelves neat and organized, papers put away

_____ Pantry organized and cleaned

_____ Private papers and mail stored, computer and printer
turned off, fax machine unplugged

_____ Broom closet organized

_____ Focal point of room clearly visible and in order

Bathrooms

_____ Attractive towels neatly displayed

_____ Sink, tub or shower, and toilet sparklingly clean

_____ Floors washed, bath mats clean and dry

_____ Dirty clothes, towels, bathrobes in the laundry

_____ Pretty soaps in the soap dish or dispenser

_____ Focal point of rooms clearly visible and in order

Bedrooms

_____ Beds made, pillows plumped, furniture straightened

_____ Dirty clothes, towels, etc., in the hamper or washing machine

_____ Clutter in your "clutter collector"

_____ Floors swept, rugs vacuumed

_____ Nightstands empty or organized attractively

_____ Focal point of rooms clearly visible and in order

Basement and Attic

_____ Floors clean and dry

_____ Mechanical systems recently serviced

_____ Toys organized, furniture straightened, boxes stacked neatly

_____ Lightbulbs working? Does the space need any additional light?

Garage

_____ Tools, bikes, garden equipment organized and safely stored

_____ Floor and stairs swept clean

Garden and Landscape

_____ Grass mowed, sidewalk and patio swept, flower beds edged

_____ Furniture stacked neatly, or organized

_____ Garbage picked up? Dishes, glasses, bottles put away

WEB SITES FOR HOME SELLERS

Web Sites change frequently, so be sure to consult my site, www.thinkglink.com, for updates and changes to this list and to items in the book, as well as for other useful information.

Building, Renovating, Remodeling, Inspecting

www.aia.org (American Institute of Architects)

www.ashi.org (American Society of Home Inspectors)

www.askbuild.com (syndicated columnist Tim Carter's Ask the Builder site)

www.nahb.com (National Association of Home Builders, Remodeling Council)

www.nari.org (National Association of the Remodeling Industry)

www.nrca.net (National Roofing Contractors Association)

www.smarthomebuy.com (property reports covering environmental hazards and other items)

Agents

www.century21.com (Century 21's national site)

www.coldwellbanker.com (Coldwell Banker's national site)

www.ERA.com (ERA's national site)

www.realtor.com (National Association of Realtors)

www.REMAX.com (RE/MAX's national site)

Seller, Credit History, Moving Information

www.bbb.org (Better Business Bureau)

www.domania.com (statistics, estimated property valuation, and other seller information)

www.ebay.com (eBay offers a home-auction site)

www.homefair.com (information on your city and schools, moving information)

www.homegain.com (HomeGain, in Emoryville, California, links sellers to agents and offers estimated valuation of your property)

www.ired.com (International Real Estate Digest, a directory of thousands of real-estate-related websites)

www.monstermoving.com (relocation and moving tips, tools and information)

www.moving.com (information for your moving day)

www.moving.org (American Moving and Storage Association)

www.myfico.com (credit histories and scores)

www.schoolmatch.com (provides information about your school district)

For Sale by Owner (FSBO)

These sites either list homes for sale by owner or offer discount brokerage services.

www.ehomes.com

www.erealty.com

www.forsalebyowner.com

www.fsbo.com

www.owners.com

www.listforless.com

www.listlow.com

www.owners.com

www.ziprealty.com

Title and Escrow Companies, Home Warranty

www.americanhomeshield.com (American Home Shield)

www.countrywide.com (Countrywide Credit, also Countrywide Home Loan, sells insurance and home warranties)

www.ctic.com or www.fnf.com (Chicago Title & Trust, also known as Fidelity National Financial)

www.firstam.com (First American Title Insurance Company)

www.quotesmith.com (sells home warranties and other insurance products)

www.stewart.com or www.landam.com (Stewart Title, also known as Land America Title)

www.ticortitle.com (Ticor Title)

Glossary of Terms

Abstract (of title)   A summary of the public records affecting the title to a particular piece of land. An attorney or title-insurance-company officer creates the abstract of title by examining all recorded instruments (documents) relating to a specific piece of property, such as easements, liens, mortgages, etc.

Acceleration clause   A provision in a loan agreement that allows the lender to require the balance of the loan to become due immediately if mortgage payments are not made or if there is a breach in your obligation under your mortgage or note.

Acquisition or bank fee   The average fee you'll pay to the dealer at the start of the lease. Typically $300 to $400, not negotiable.

Addendum   Any addition to, or modification of, a contract. Also called an *amendment* or *rider*.

Adjustable-rate mortgage (ARM)   A type of loan whose prevailing interest rate is tied to an economic index (like one-year Treasury notes), which fluctuates with the market. There are three types of ARMs, including one-year ARMs, which adjust every year; three-year ARMs, which adjust every three years; and five-year ARMs, which adjust every five years. When the loan adjusts, the lender tacks a margin onto the economic index rate to come up with your loan's new rate. ARMs are considered far riskier than fixed-rate mortgages, but their starting interest rates are extremely low, and in the past five to ten years, people have done very well with them.

Agency   A term used to describe the relationship between a seller and a broker, or a buyer and a broker.

Agency closing The lender's use of a title company or other party to act on the lender's behalf for the purposes of closing on the purchase of a home or refinancing a loan.

Agent An individual who represents a buyer or a seller in the purchase or sale of a home. Licensed by the state, an agent must work for a broker or a brokerage firm.

Agreement of sale This document is also known as the *contract to purchase, purchase agreement,* or *sales agreement.* It is the agreement by which the seller agrees to sell you his or her property if you pay a certain price. It contains all the provisions and conditions for the purchase, must be written, and is signed by both parties.

Amortization A payment plan that enables the borrower to reduce his debt gradually through monthly payments of principal and interest. Amortization tables allow you to see exactly how much you would pay each month in interest and how much you repay in principal, depending on the amount of money borrowed at a specific interest rate.

Annual percentage rate (APR) The total cost of your loan, expressed as a percentage rate of interest, which includes not only the loan's interest rate, but also factors in all the costs associated with making that loan, including closing costs and fees. The costs are then amortized over the life of the loan. Banks are required by the federal Truth-in-Lending statutes to disclose the APR of a loan, which allows borrowers a common ground for comparing various loans from different lenders.

Application A series of documents you must fill out when you apply for a loan.

Application fee A onetime fee charged by the mortgage company for processing your application for a loan. Sometimes the application fee is applied toward certain costs, including the appraisal and credit report.

Appraisal The opinion of an appraiser, who estimates the value of a home at a specific point in time.

Articles-of-agreement mortgage A type of seller financing that allows the buyer to purchase the home in installments over a specified period of time. The seller keeps legal title to the home until the loan is paid off. The buyer receives an interest in the property—called *equitable title*—but does not own it. However, because the buyer is paying the real-estate taxes and paying interest to the seller, it is the buyer who receives the tax benefits of home ownership.

Assumption of mortgage If you assume a mortgage when you purchase a home, you undertake to fulfill the obligations of the existing loan agreement the seller made with the lender. The obligations are similar to those that you would incur if you took out a new mortgage. When assuming a mortgage, you become personally liable for the payment of principal and interest. The seller, or original mortgagor, is released from the liability, and should get that release in writing. Otherwise, he or she could be liable if you don't make the monthly payments.

Balloon mortgage A type of mortgage that is generally short in length, but is amortized over twenty-five or thirty years so that the borrower pays a combination of interest and principal each month. At the end of the loan term, the entire balance of the loan must be repaid at once.

Broker An individual who acts as the agent of the seller or the buyer. A real-estate broker must be licensed by the state.

Building line or setback The distance from the front, back, or side of a lot beyond which construction or improvements may not extend without permission by the proper governmental authority. The building line may be established by a filed plat of subdivision, by restrictive covenants in deeds, by building codes, or by zoning ordinances.

Buy down An incentive offered by a developer or a seller that allows the buyer to lower his or her initial interest rate by putting up a certain amount of money. A buy down also refers to the process of paying extra points up front at the closing of your loan in order to have a lower interest rate over the life of the loan.

Buyer broker   A buyer broker is a real-estate broker who specializes in representing buyers. Unlike a seller broker or a conventional broker, the buyer broker has a fiduciary duty to the buyer, because the buyer accepts the legal obligation of paying the broker. The buyer broker is obligated to find the best property for a client, and then negotiate the best possible purchase price and terms. Buyer brokerage has gained a significant amount of respect in recent years, since the National Association of Realtors has changed its code of ethics to accept this designation.

Buyer's market   Market conditions that favor the buyer. A buyer's market is usually expressed when there are too many homes for sale, and a home can be bought for less money.

Certificate of title   A document or instrument issued by a local government agency to a homeowner, naming the homeowner as the owner of a specific piece of property. At the sale of the property, the certificate of title is transferred to the buyer. The agency then issues a new certificate of title to the buyer.

Chain of title   The lineage of ownership of a particular property.

Closing   The day when buyers and sellers sign the papers and actually swap money for title to the new home. The closing finalizes the agreements reached in the sales agreement.

Closing costs   This phrase can refer to a lender's costs for closing on a loan, or it can mean all the costs associated with closing on a piece of property. Considering all closing costs, it's easy to see that closing can be expensive for both buyers and sellers. A home buyer's closing costs might include lender's points; loan origination or loan service fees; loan application fee; lender's credit report; lender's processing fee; lender's document preparation fee; lender's appraisal fee; prepaid interest on the loan; lender's insurance escrow; lender's real-estate-tax escrow; lender's tax escrow service fee; cost for the lender's title policy; special endorsements to the lender's title policy; house inspection fees; title company closing fee; deed or mortgage recording fees; local municipal, county, and state taxes; and the attorney's fee. A seller's closing costs might include the survey (which in some parts of the country is paid for by the buyer); title insurance; recorded release of mortgage; broker's commission; state, county, and local municipality transfer taxes; credit to the buyer for unpaid real-estate taxes and other bills; attorney's fees; and FHA fees and costs.

Cloud (on title)   An outstanding claim or encumbrance that adversely affects the marketability of a property.

Commission   The amount of money paid to the broker by the seller (or, in some cases, the buyer), as compensation for selling the home. Usually, the commission is a percentage of the sales price of the home, and generally hovers in the 5 to 7 percent range. There is no "set" commission rate. It is always and entirely negotiable.

Condemnation   The government holds the right to "condemn" land for public use, even against the will of the owner. The government, however, must pay fair market price for the land. Condemnation may also mean that the government has decided a particular piece of land, or a dwelling, is unsafe for human habitation.

Condominium   A dwelling of two or more units in which you individually own the interior space of your unit and jointly own common areas such as the lobby, roof, parking, plumbing, and recreational areas.

Contingency   A provision in a contract that sets forth one or more conditions that must be met prior to the closing. If the contingency is not met, usually the party who is benefiting from the contingency can terminate the contract. Some common contingencies include financing, inspection, attorney approval, and toxic substances.

Contract to purchase   Another name for *agreement of sale*.

Contractor   In the building industry, the contractor is the individual who contracts to build the property. He or she erects the structure and manages the subcontracting (to the electrician, plumber, etc.) until the project is finished.

Conventional mortgage   A conventional mortgage is a loan that is underwritten by banks, savings and loans, or other types of mortgage companies. There are also certain limitations imposed on conventional mortgages that allow them to be sold to private institutional investors (like pension funds) on the secondary market. For example, as of 2002, the loan must be less than $300,700, otherwise it is considered a "jumbo" loan. Also, if you are buying a condominium, conventional financing decrees that the condo building be more than 70 percent owner-occupied.

Co-op   Cooperative housing refers to a building, or a group of buildings, owned by a corporation. The shareholders of the corporation are the people who live in the building. They own shares—which gives them the right to lease a specific unit within the building—in the corporation that owns their building and pay "rent" or monthly maintenance assessments for the expenses associated with living in the building. Co-ops are relatively unknown outside of New York, Chicago, and a few other cities. Since the 1970s, condominiums have become much more popular.

Counteroffer   When the seller or buyer responds to a bid. If you decide to offer $100,000 for a home listed at $150,000, the seller might counter your offer and propose that you purchase the home for $140,000. That new proposal, and any subsequent offer, is called a counteroffer.

Covenant   Assurances or promises set out in the deed or a legally binding contract, or implied in the law. For example, when you obtain title to a property by warranty, there is the covenant of quiet enjoyment, which gives you the right to enjoy your property without disturbances.

Credit report   A lender will decide whether to give you a loan based on your credit history. A credit report lists all of your credit accounts (such as charge cards), and any debts or late payments that have been reported to the credit company.

Cul-de-sac   A street that ends in a U-shape, leading the driver or pedestrian back to the beginning. The cul-de-sac has become exceptionally popular with modern subdivision developers, who use the design technique to create quiet streets and give the development a nonlinear feel.

Custom builder   A home builder who builds houses for individual owners to the owners' specification. The home builder may either own a piece of property or build a home on someone else's land.

Debt service   The total amount of debt (credit cards, mortgage, car loan) that an individual is carrying at any one time.

Declaration of restrictions   Developers of condominiums (or any other type of housing unit that functions as a condo) are required to file a condominium declaration, which sets out the rules and restrictions for the property, the division of ownership, and the rights and privileges of the owners. The "condo dec." or "home owner's dec.," as it is commonly called, reflects the developer's original intent, and may only be changed by unit-owner vote. There are other types of declarations, including those for homeowners' associations and town-house associations. Co-op dwellers are governed by a similar type of document.

Deed   The document used to transfer ownership in a property from seller to buyer.

Deed of trust   A deed of trust, or *trust deed*, is an instrument similar to a mortgage that gives the lender the right to foreclose on the property if there is a default under the trust deed or note by the borrower.

Deposit   Money given by the buyer to the seller with a signed contract to purchase or offer to purchase, as a show of good faith. Also called the *earnest money*.

Down payment   The cash put into a purchase by the borrower. Lenders like to see the borrower put at least 20 percent down in cash, because lenders generally believe that if you have a higher cash down payment, it is less likely the home will go into foreclosure. In recent years, however, lenders have become more flexible about cash down payments; recently, lenders have begun accepting cash down payments of as little as 5 percent.

Dual agency   When a real-estate broker represents both the buyer and the seller in a single transaction it creates a situation known as dual agency. In most states, brokers must disclose to the buyer and to the seller whom they are representing. Even with disclosure, dual agency presents a conflict of interest for the broker in the transaction. If the broker is acting as the seller broker and the subagent for the seller (by bringing the buyer), then anything the buyer tells the broker must, by law, be brought to the seller's attention. If the broker represents the seller as a seller broker and the buyer as a buyer broker in the same transaction, the broker will receive money from both the buyer and the seller, an obvious conflict of interest.

Due on sale clause   Nearly every mortgage has this clause, which states that the mortgage must be paid off in full upon the sale of the home.

Earnest money   The money the buyer gives the seller up front as a show of good faith. It can be as much as 10 percent of the purchase price. Earnest money is sometimes called a *deposit.*

Easement   A right given by a landowner to a third party to make use of the land in a specific way. There may be several easements on your property, including for passage of utility lines or poles, sewer or water mains, and even a driveway. Once the right is given, it continues indefinitely, or until released by the party who received it.

Eminent domain   The right of the government to condemn private land for public use. The government must, however, pay full market value for the property.

Encroachment   When your neighbor builds a garage or a fence, and it occupies your land, it is said to "encroach on" your property.

Encumbrance   A claim or lien or interest in a property by another party. An encumbrance hinders the seller's ability to pass good, marketable, and unencumbered title to you.

Escrow closing   A third party, usually a title company, acts as the neutral party for the receipt of documents for the exchange of the deed by the seller for the buyer's money. The final exchange is completed when the third party determines that certain preset requirements have been satisfied.

Escrow (for earnest money)   The document that creates the arrangement whereby a third party or broker holds the earnest money for the benefit of the buyer and the seller.

Escrow (for real-estate taxes and insurance)   An account in which monthly installments for real-estate taxes and property insurance are held—usually in the name of the home buyer's lender.

Fee simple   The most basic type of ownership, under which the owner has the right to use and dispose of the property at will.

Fiduciary duty   A relationship of trust between a broker and a seller or a buyer broker and a buyer, or an attorney and a client.

First mortgage   A mortgage that takes priority over all other voluntary liens.

Fixture   Personal property, such as a built-in bookcase, furnace, hot-water heater, and recessed lights, that becomes "affixed" because it has been permanently attached to the home.

Foreclosure   The legal action taken to extinguish a homeowner's right and interest in a property, so that the property can be sold in a foreclosure sale to satisfy a debt.

Gift letter   A letter to the lender indicating that a gift of cash has been made to the buyer and that it is not expected to be repaid. The letter must detail the amount of the gift, and the name of the giver.

Good faith estimate (GFE)   Under the Real Estate Settlement Procedures Act, or RESPA, lenders are required to give potential borrowers a written good faith estimate of closing costs within three days of an application submission.

Grace period   The period of time after a loan payment due date in which a mortgage payment may be made and not be considered delinquent.

Graduated payment mortgage   A mortgage in which the payments increase over the life of the mortgage, allowing the borrower to make very low payments at the beginning of the loan.

Hazard insurance   Insurance that covers the property from damages that might materially affect its value. Also known as *homeowner's insurance*.

Holdback   An amount of money held back at closing by the lender or the escrow agent until a particular condition has been met. If the problem is a repair, the money is kept until the repair is made. If the repair is not made, the lender or escrow agent uses the money to make the repair. Buyers and sellers may also have holdbacks between them, to ensure that specific conditions of the sale are met.

Homeowner's association   A group of homeowners in a particular subdivision or area who band together to take care of common property and common interests.

Homeowner's insurance   Coverage that includes hazard insurance, as well as personal liability and theft.

Home warranty   A service contract that covers appliances (with exclusions) in working condition in the home for a certain period of time, usually one year. Homeowners are responsible for a per-call service fee. Another type of warranty exists for new construction. Some developers will purchase a warranty from a company specializing in new construction for the homes they sell. A home warranty will warrant the good working order of the appliances and workmanship of a new home for between one and ten years; for example, appliances might be covered for one year while the roof may be covered for several years.

Housing and Urban Development, Department of   Also known as HUD, this is the federal department responsible for the nation's housing programs. It also regulates RESPA, the Real Estate Settlement Procedures Act, which governs how lenders must deal with their customers.

Inspection   The service an inspector performs when he or she is hired to scrutinize the home for any possible structural defects. May also be done in order to check for the presence of toxic substances, such as leaded paint or water, asbestos, radon, or pests, including termites.

Installment contract   The purchase of property in installments. Title to the property is given to the purchaser when all installments are made.

Institutional investors or lenders   Private or public companies, corporations, or funds (such as pension funds) that purchase loans on the secondary market from commercial lenders such as banks and savings and loans; or, they are sources of funds for mortgages through mortgage brokers.

Interest   Money charged for the use of borrowed funds. Usually expressed as an interest rate, it is the percentage of the total loan charged annually for the use of the funds.

Interest-only mortgage   A loan in which only the interest is paid on a regular basis (usually monthly), and the principal is owed in full at the end of the loan term.

Interest Rate Cap   The total number of percentage points that an adjustable-rate mortgage (ARM) might rise over the life of the loan.

Joint tenancy   An equal, undivided ownership in a property taken by two or more owners. Under joint tenancy there are rights of survivorship, which means that if one of the owners dies, the surviving owner rather than the heirs of the estate inherits the other's total interest in the property.

Landscape The trees, flowers, plantings, lawn, and shrubbery that surround the exterior of a dwelling.

Late charge A penalty applied to a mortgage payment that arrives after the grace period (usually the tenth or fifteenth of a month).

Lease with an option to buy A lease that gives the renter or lessee of a piece of property the right to purchase the property for a specific period of time at a specific price. Usually, a lease with an option to buy allows a first-time buyer to accumulate a down payment by applying a portion of the monthly rent toward the down payment.

Lender A person, company, corporation, or entity that lends money for the purchase of real estate.

Letter of intent A formal statement, usually in letter form, from the buyer to the seller stating that the buyer intends to purchase a specific piece of property for a specific price on a specific date.

Leverage Using a small amount of cash, say a 10 or 20 percent down payment, to purchase a piece of property.

Lien An encumbrance against the property, which may be voluntary or involuntary. There are many different kinds of liens, including a tax lien (for unpaid federal, state, or real-estate taxes), a judgment lien (for monetary judgments by a court of law), a mortgage lien (when you take out a mortgage), and a mechanic's lien (for work done by a contractor on the property that has not been paid for). For a lien to be attached to the property's title, it must be filed or recorded with local county government.

Listing A property that a broker agrees to list for sale in return for a commission.

Loan An amount of money that is lent to a borrower, who agrees to repay it plus interest.

Loan commitment A written document that states that a mortgage company has agreed to lend a buyer a certain amount of money at a certain rate of interest for a specific period of time, which may contain sets of conditions and a date by which the loan must close.

Loan origination fee   A onetime fee charged by the mortgage company to arrange the financing for the loan.

Loan-to-value ratio   The ratio of the amount of money you wish to borrow compared to the value of the property you wish to purchase. Institutional investors (who buy loans on the secondary market from your mortgage company) set up certain ratios that guide lending practices. For example, the mortgage company might only lend you 80 percent of a property's value.

Location   Where property is geographically situated. "Location, location, location" is a broker's maxim that states where the property is located is its most important feature, because you can change everything about a house, except its location.

Lock-in   The mechanism by which a borrower locks in the interest rate that will be charged on a particular loan. Usually, the lock lasts for a certain time period, such as thirty, forty-five, or sixty days. On a new construction, the lock may be much longer.

Maintenance fee   The monthly or annual fee charged to condo, co-op, or town-house owners, and paid to the homeowner's association, for the maintenance of common property. Also called an assessment.

Mortgage   A document granting a lien on a home in exchange for financing granted by a lender. The mortgage is the means by which the lender secures the loan and has the ability to foreclose on the home.

Mortgage banker   A company or a corporation, like a bank, that lends its own funds to borrowers in addition to bringing together lenders and borrowers. A mortgage banker may also service the loan (that is, collect the monthly payments).

Mortgage broker   A company or individual that brings together lenders and borrowers and processes mortgage applications.

Mortgagee   A legal term for the lender.

Mortgagor   A legal term for the borrower.

Multiple listing service (MLS)   A computerized listing of all properties offered for sale by member brokers. Buyers may only gain access to the MLS by working with a member broker.

Negative amortization   A condition created when the monthly mortgage payment is less than the amount necessary to pay off the loan over the period of time set forth in the note. Because you're paying less than the amount necessary, the actual loan amount increases over time. That's how you end up with negative equity. To pay off the loan, a lump-sum payment must be made.

Option   When a buyer pays for the right, or option, to purchase property for a given length of time without having the obligation to actually purchase the property.

Origination fee   A fee charged by the lender for allowing you to borrow money to purchase property. The fee—which is also referred to as *points*—is usually expressed as a percentage of the total loan amount.

Ownership   The absolute right to use, enjoy, and dispose of property. You own it!

Package mortgage   A mortgage that uses both real and personal property to secure a loan.

Paper   Slang that refers to the mortgage, trust deed, installment, and land contract.

Personal property   Movable property, such as appliances, furniture, clothing, and artwork.

PITI   An acronym for *principal, interest, taxes, and insurance*. These are usually the four parts of your monthly mortgage payment.

Pledged account   Borrowers who do not want to have a real-estate tax or insurance escrow administered by the mortgage servicer can, in some circumstances, pledge a savings account into which enough money to cover real-estate taxes and the insurance premium must be deposited. You must then make the payments for your real-estate taxes and insurance premiums from a separate account. If you fail to pay your taxes or premiums, the lender is allowed to use the funds in the pledged account to make those payments.

Point   A point is 1 percent of the loan amount.

Possession   Being in control of a piece of property, and having the right to use it to the exclusion of all others.

Power of attorney   The legal authorization given to an individual to act on behalf of another individual.

Prepaid interest   Interest paid at closing for the number of days left in the month after closing. For example, if you close on the fifteenth, you would prepay the interest for the sixteenth through the end of the month.

Prepayment penalty   A fine imposed when a loan is paid off before it comes due. Many states now have laws against prepayment penalties, although banks with federal charters are exempt from state laws. If possible, do not use a mortgage that has a prepayment penalty, or you will be charged a fine if you sell your property before your mortgage has been paid off.

Prequalifying for a loan   When a mortgage company tells a buyer in advance of the formal application approximately how much money the buyer can afford to borrow.

Principal   The amount of money you borrow.

Private mortgage insurance (PMI)   Special insurance that specifically protects the top 20 percent of a loan, allowing the lender to lend more than 80 percent of the value of the property. PMI is paid in monthly installments by the borrower.

Property tax   A tax levied by a county or a local authority on the value of real estate.

Proration   The proportional division of certain costs of home ownership. Usually used at closing to figure out how much the buyer and seller each owe for certain expenditures, including real-estate taxes, assessments, and water bills.

Purchase agreement   An agreement between the buyer and the seller for the purchase of property.

Purchase money mortgage   An instrument used in seller financing, a purchase money mortgage is signed by a buyer and given to the seller in exchange for a portion of the purchase price.

Quit-claim deed   A deed that operates to release any interest in a property that a person may have, *without a representation that he or she actually has a right in that property.* For example, Sally may use a quit-claim deed to grant Bill her interest in the White House, in Washington, D.C., although she may not actually own, or have any rights to, that particular house.

Real estate   Land and anything permanently attached to it, such as buildings and improvements.

Real-estate agent   An individual licensed by the state, who acts on behalf of the seller or the buyer. For his or her services, the agent receives a commission, which is usually expressed as a percentage of the sales price of a home and is split with his or her real-estate firm. A real-estate agent must either be a real-estate broker or work for one.

Real-estate attorney   An attorney who specializes in the purchase and sale of real estate.

Real-estate broker   An individual who is licensed by the state to act as an agent on behalf of the seller or the buyer. For his or her services, the broker receives a commission, which is usually expressed as a percentage of the sales price of a home.

Real Estate Settlement Procedures Act (RESPA)   This federal statute was originally passed in 1974, and contains provisions that govern the way companies involved with a real-estate closing must treat each other and the consumer. For example, one section of RESPA requires lenders to give consumers a written good faith estimate within three days of making an application for a loan. Another section of RESPA prohibits title companies from giving referral fees to brokers for steering business to them.

Realtist   A designation given to an agent or broker who is a member of the National Association of Real Estate Brokers.

Realtor   A designation given to a real-estate agent or broker who is a member of the National Association of Realtors.

Recording   The process of filing documents at a specific government office. Upon such recording, the document becomes part of the public record.

Redlining   The slang term used to describe an illegal practice of discrimination against a particular racial group by real-estate lenders. Redlining occurs when lenders decide certain areas of a community are too high risk and refuse to lend to buyers who want to purchase property in those areas, regardless of their qualifications or creditworthiness.

Regulation M   The revised federal rules that went into effect at the end of 1997. Regulation M standardized and simplified leasing forms and language. While it requires dealers to disclose all sorts of information, it does not require them to disclose the money factor (also known as the lease rate).

Regulation Z   Also known as the Truth-in-Lending Act. Congress determined that lenders must provide a written good faith estimate of closing costs to all borrowers and provide them with other written information about the loan.

Reserve   The amount of money set aside by a condo, co-op, or homeowners' association for future capital improvements.

Sale-leaseback   A transaction in which the seller sells property to a buyer, who then leases the property back to the seller. This is accomplished within the same transaction.

Sales contract   The document by which a buyer contracts to purchase property. Also known as the purchase contract or a *contract to purchase.*

Second mortgage   A mortgage that is obtained after the primary mortgage, and whose rights for repayment are secondary to the first mortgage.

Seller broker A broker who has a fiduciary responsibility to the seller. Most brokers are seller brokers, although an increasing number are buyer brokers, who have a fiduciary responsibility to the buyer.

Settlement statement A statement that details the monies paid out and received by the buyer and the seller at closing.

Shared appreciation mortgage A relatively new mortgage used to help first-time buyers who might not qualify for conventional financing. In a shared appreciation mortgage, the lender offers a below-market interest rate in return for a portion of the profits made by the homeowner when the property is sold. Before entering into a shared appreciation mortgage, be sure to have your real-estate attorney review the documentation.

Special assessment An additional charge levied by a condo or co-op board in order to pay for capital improvements, or other unforeseen expenses.

Subagent A broker who brings the buyer to the property. Although subagents would appear to be working for the buyer (a subagent usually ferries around the buyer, showing him or her properties), they are paid by the seller and have a fiduciary responsibility to the seller. Subagency is often confusing to first-time buyers, who think that because the subagent shows them property, the subagent is "their" agent, rather than the seller's.

Subdivision The division of a large piece of property into several smaller pieces. Usually a developer or a group of developers will build single-family or duplex homes of a similar design and cost within one subdivision.

Tax lien A lien that is attached to property if the owner does not pay his or her real-estate taxes or federal income taxes. If overdue property taxes are not paid, the owner's property might be sold at auction for the amount owed in back taxes.

Tenancy by the entirety A type of ownership whereby both the husband and the wife each own the complete property. Each spouse has an ownership interest in the property as their marital residence and, as a result, creditors cannot force the sale of the home to pay back the debts of one spouse without the other spouse's consent. There are rights of survivorship whereby upon the death of one spouse, the other spouse would immediately inherit the entire property.

Tenants in common   A type of ownership in which two or more parties have an undivided interest in the property. The owners may or may not have equal shares of ownership, and there are no rights of survivorship. However, each owner retains the right to sell his or her share in the property as he or she sees fit.

Title   Refers to the ownership of a particular piece of property.

Title company   The corporation or company that insures the status of title (title insurance) through the closing, and may handle other aspects of the closing.

Title insurance   Insurance that protects the lender and the property owner against losses arising from defects or problems with the title to property.

Torrens title   A system of recording the chain of ownership for property, which takes its name from the man who created it in Australia in 1858, Sir Robert Torrens. While that system was popular in the nineteenth century, most cities have converted to other, less cumbersome, systems of recording.

Trust account   An account used by brokers and escrow agents, in which funds for another individual are held separately, and not commingled with other funds.

Underwriter   One who underwrites a loan for another. Your lender will have an investor underwrite your loan.

Variable interest rate   An interest rate that rises and falls according to a particular economic indicator, such as Treasury notes.

Void   A contract or document that is not enforceable.

Voluntary lien   A lien, such as a mortgage, that a homeowner elects to grant to a lender.

Waiver   The surrender or relinquishment of a particular right, claim, or privilege.

Warranty   A legally binding promise given to the buyer at closing by the seller, generally regarding the condition of the home, property, or other matter.

Zoning   The right of the local municipal government to decide how different areas of the municipality will be used. Zoning ordinances are the laws that govern the use of the land.

Acknowledgments

Over the past fifteen years that I have been writing about money and real estate, I have interviewed thousands of home buyers, sellers, owners, agents, lenders, and other people involved with the process of buying, selling, financing, living in, and closing on homes. I am deeply grateful to everyone who has been so open and frank, sharing stories about their successes and failures, triumphs and mistakes, satisfactions and frustrations. I have included the best of what I have learned from them in this book, and while I have faithfully retold their stories, in some cases I have changed their names or the cities in which these individuals live.

There is no way I could do it all without the help of my assistant, April Powell, and intern, Jennifer Catlin, who work hard to keep me, and all of the research for my books, as organized as possible. My former Three Rivers Press editor, Betsy Rapoport, fell in love with this book (even though she had just completed renovating her home and had no intention of moving), and her successor, Annik LaFarge, who also has no plans to move (ever!), picked up the torch and carried forward, helping to shape the final draft of this manuscript. Dori Steele always has an answer, and Brian Belfiglio makes magical things happen with the media. Thank you. My agent and friend, Alice Martell, always encourages me and is the world's best New York lunch date.

My family delights in the publication of each new book, and supports me in this crazy business of helping consumers make smart choices for themselves. I could not do it without them.

But most of all, I am grateful for the unwavering support of my husband and best friend, Sam, the world's best real-estate attorney and editor, who continues to believe my wildest dreams will come true.

Index

ABOUT THE AUTHOR

ILYCE R. GLINK's newspaper column, "Real Estate Matters," is syndicated nationally. She is the money and real estate reporter for WGN-TV in Chicago, guest host for *The Clark Howard Show* on WSB-AM in Atlanta, and has appeared on *Oprah* and the *Today* show. Her books include *100 Questions You Should Ask About Your Personal Finances, 100 Questions Every First-Time Home Buyer Should Ask,* and *50 Simple Steps You Can Take to Disaster-Proof Your Finances.* She lives in the Chicago area with her husband and two sons.

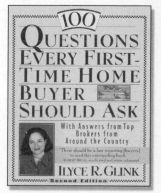
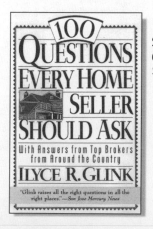